THE GOLDEN BOOK OF TILLOTSON

The Golden Book of Tillotson

SELECTIONS FROM THE WRITINGS OF
THE REV. JOHN TILLOTSON, D.D.
ARCHBISHOP OF CANTERBURY

Edited, with a Sketch of his Life,

BY

JAMES MOFFATT, D.D., D.Litt.
Hon. M.A. (Oxon)

GREENWOOD PRESS, PUBLISHERS
WESTPORT, CONNECTICUT

Originally published in 1926
by Hodder and Stoughton, Ltd., London

First Greenwood Reprinting 1971

Library of Congress Catalogue Card Number 72-109866

SBN 8371-4357-8

Printed in the United States of America

CONTENTS

CONTENTS

CONTENTS

'Tillotson was a man of a clear head and a sweet temper. He had the brightest thoughts and the most correct style of all our divines, and was esteemed the best preacher of the age. . . . He was eminent for his opposition to popery; he was no friend to persecution, and he stood up much against atheism: nor did any man contribute more to bring the city to love our worship than he did. But there was so little superstition and so much reason and gentleness in his way of explaining things, that malice was long levelled at him, and in conclusion broke in fiercely on him.'—BURNET, *The History of My Own Time*, Book I. chapter vi.

'There was as complete anarchy in the prose as in the religion of the land; and so the calm, equable, harmonious, idiomatic sentences of Tillotson, his plain, practical theology, fell as a grateful relief upon the English ear and heart. Tillotson must be taken with his age; and if we can throw ourselves back upon his age, we shall comprehend the mastery which he held, for a century at least, over the religion and over the literature of the country.'—MILMAN, *Annals of St. Paul's Cathedral*, p. 421.

'Tillotson still keeps his place as a legitimate English classic. His highest flights were indeed far below those of Taylor, of Barrow, and of South; but his oratory was more correct and equable than theirs. . . . There is about his manner a certain graceful ease which marks him as a man who knows the world, who has lived in populous cities and in splendid courts, and who has conversed, not only with books, but with lawyers and merchants, wits and beauties, statesmen and princes. The greatest charm of his compositions, however, is derived from the benignity and candour which appear in every line, and which shone forth not less conspicuously in his life than in his writings.'—MACAULAY, *The History of England*, chapter xiv.

'Tillotson did for his own time the work that was most needful in the way that was most suitable. After the orgies of the saints and the orgies of the sinners, he made sanity acceptable to a whole generation.'—DOWDEN, *Puritan and Anglican*, p. 326.

'Il ne ressemble pas à ces prédicateurs français, académiciens, beaux diseurs, qui par un air de cœur, par un Advent bien prêché, par les finesses d'un style épuré, gagnent le premier évêché vacant et la faveur de la bonne compagnie. Mais il écrit en parfait honnête homme, on voit qu'il ne cherche point du tout la gloire d'orateur; il veut persuader solidement, rien de plus. On jouit de cette clarté, de ce naturel, de cette justesse, de cette loyauté entière.'— H. TAINE, *Histoire de la littérature anglaise*, Book III. ch. iii.

TILLOTSON AND HIS TIMES

I

'WE are incomparably the greatest county in England,' said Tillotson once, addressing a gathering of Yorkshiremen. He was justly proud of belonging to no mean county in England. Unlike two of his older contemporaries, Bishop Sanderson and Andrew Marvell, both Yorkshiremen, he lived through not only the Civil War and the Restoration, but also the Revolution of 1689, which really ended the seventeenth century. Tillotson was born in the same year as John Howe and as Isaac Barrow, the notable mathematician and theologian, whose works he helped to edit for the press. He was one year older than Dryden, two years older than Locke, three years older than Pepys, Halifax, and South ; Bunyan and Sir William Temple were his seniors by two years, George Fox by six ; Stilling-fleet was five years younger, Ken seven.

Tillotson's father was a prosperous clothier in Sowerby, who gave his son a sound education and sent him, at the age of seventeen, to Cambridge. Trinity was the college of Barrow and Dryden, but young Tillotson went to Clare Hall. It was not in a prosperous condition when he was an under-graduate ; the buildings were still unfinished, and several of the fellows had been ejected for refusing to comply with the Puritan régime; indeed, it had no Master till 1650, when Cudworth took charge of it for four years. Tillotson studied conscientiously, and on becoming a tutor showed a deep interest in the religious welfare of his pupils. He kept in line still with the traditions of the Calvinistic Puritanism in which he had been trained at home. His favourite preachers at Cambridge were Presbyterians. But wider influences were beginning to play upon his mind as he matured. There is no doubt, for example, that Chillingworth's broad treatise, *The Religion of Protestants a Safe Way to Salvation* (1637), impressed him. And he grew by meeting men as well as by reading books. The movement of religious humanism in the University touched him. Jeremy Taylor, it is true, had left for Oxford in 1635, but a group of men were teaching in Cambridge who represented a distinctive philosophy of religion; Whichcote was Provost of King's, Patrick and John Smith were fellows of Queens', Henry More was a fellow of Christ's, and Tillotson's friend Stillingfleet was a scholar of St. John's. Tillotson was not a disciple of these Cambridge Platonists either then or afterwards; he had no sympathy with their mystical fervour and spiritual intuitions. But he did learn from them the truth that man's reason is capable of understanding the principles of natural and revealed religion. When he left Cambridge, he was a young man who, like Whichcote and Locke, had begun to outgrow the narrower Puritanism in which he had been born and bred.

But as yet there was no outward break. When he went up to London about 1656, he became tutor to the son of Sir Edmund Prideaux, Cromwell's Attorney-General, acting as chaplain in the household. Two other Cambridge men were in London at the same time, Marvell and Dryden, both connected with what roughly corresponds to the modern Foreign Office. They presently rolled off into politics and poetry, but though Tillotson was still undecided in his ecclesiastical views, he was facing a clerical career. The Civil War had broken out when he was a schoolboy; Charles the First had been executed when he was an undergraduate; he was in London when Cromwell died on September 3, 1658, and one experience at this period shows how he was detaching himself from the extremer Puritan party. He told Burnet how he chanced to be at Whitehall a week after the Protector's death, and found a religious service for the family being conducted by several leading Puritans, including Thomas Goodwin and John Owen. The tone of the prayers disgusted him. ' God was as it were reproached with Cromwell's services, and challenged for taking him away so soon. Goodwin, who had pretended to assure them in a prayer that he was not to die, which was but a very few minutes before he expired, had the impudence to say to God, *Thou hast deceived us, and we are deceived.* Sterry, praying for Richard, used those indecent words, next to blasphemy, *Make him the brightness of the father's glory, and the express image of his person.'* It cannot have been the use of extemporary prayer that repelled Tillotson, for he was known to have a gift of such prayer himself. The unfavourable impression which the incident made on his mind must have been due to the fact that he had already become critical of the Puritan position and disposed to take a wider view of religion, which was neither Laudian nor Puritan. One of the books which drew him over to moderate Anglicanism was Stillingfleet's *Irenicon*, published in 1659, with its presentation of Church Government as immaterial and of Episcopacy as suitable but not absolutely essential. ' As this was never seriously answered, it was accepted as a standing refutation of the High episcopalian theory.' [1]   Such views, combined with the intercourse which he eventually enjoyed with men like Dr. John Wilkins, now Master of Trinity, enabled Tillotson eventually to adhere to the Church of England as his spiritual home.

His ordination was curious. There was in London the only surviving bishop of the Scottish Church, Dr. Thomas Sydserf of Galloway. According to Burnet, this prelate, ' with others of the Scottish clergy gathered round him, set up a very indefensible practice of ordaining all those of the English clergy who came to him, and that without demanding either oaths or subscription from them.'

[1] Gwatkin, *Church and State in England to the Death of Queen Anne*, p. 391.

Tillotson seems to have taken orders thus. But he still kept on friendly terms with the moderate Puritans, hoping to avoid a bitter breach between them and the rigid party. Thus one of his first sermons was preached at Oswaldkirk, in Yorkshire, for his Puritan college friend, Denton, who was ejected from that living in 1662 for Nonconformity. He was also present with the Presbyterian commissioners at the Savoy Conference of 1661, from which so much was expected and so little resulted in the shape of godly concord. It is disputed whether Ken was the author of the treatise called *Ichabod*, which appeared in 1663, but at any rate this pled for sympathetic treatment of the ' sad race of dissenters ' at the hands of loyal Anglicans, which was Tillotson's desire, then and always. Even later, in 1675 and 1680, he and Stillingfleet tried to come to terms with the more moderate Nonconformist leaders like Howe and Baxter, but the spirit of the age was against reconciling measures between the high-flying party in the Church and the equally obstinate dissenters. Tillotson's aims and fortunes were oddly like those of his Scottish contemporary, Archbishop Leighton. Both showed Christian forbearance towards opponents who maligned them for being unsound and latitudinarian ; both worked generously if not wisely for some accommodation between the Episcopal and the Presbyterian parties, and both had at heart the reunion of Protestant Christians. Unluckily the divisive forces were stronger than the spirit of conciliation south as well as north of the Border. What wrecked Tillotson's project in the long run was the Act of Uniformity in 1662, a harsh and regrettable measure by which the Puritans were punished for their dealings with the Church during the brief day of their authority. They had excluded non-Puritans from a share in the government of the country, and had prohibited the Prayer Book. Now the Anglican Parliament and Church enforced ' unfeigned consent and assent ' to the Prayer Book. The loss did not yet seem irreparable, however, and to the end Tillotson tried to discover some *via media*. As late as 1685, with the sanction of Archbishop Sancroft, he worked for concessions to the dissenters, but the question of reordination usually proved the stumbling-block. Unreasonable scruples were met with an insolent impatience ; the larger charity of the broader-minded men on both sides could not accomplish anything against the clashing tempers of the day. Still, Tillotson retained a genuine respect for men whose conscientious objections he could not adopt, but for whose Christian spirit he had nothing but sincere admiration. One example may be quoted to show how he had an understanding with the more reasonable Nonconformists. In 1677, when Dr. William Lloyd was appointed vicar of St. Martin-in-the-Fields, Baxter tells us, ' I was encouraged by Dr. Tillotson to offer him my chapel in Oxenden Street for public worship, which he accepted, to my great satisfaction. And now there is constant preaching there.

Be it by Conformists or Nonconformists, I rejoice that Christ is preached to the people in that parish, whom ten or twenty such chapels cannot hold.' Dr. Lloyd was a man after Tillotson's heart, a staunch Protestant, with Puritan Catholic sympathies.

II

However, this is to anticipate.

In 1661, soon after his ordination, he became curate at Cheshunt in Hertfordshire, where he began already to justify the high hopes entertained of him by prominent Churchmen. His remarkable gift of preaching attracted notice, and promotion came quickly. He was appointed rector of Kedington in Suffolk. The local congregation, however, were accustomed to more definitely Puritan language from the pulpit, and fortunately for Tillotson his stay in this parish was brief. His growing reputation as a preacher brought him in 1663 to Lincoln's Inn as chaplain, a distinguished post which had been held earlier in the century by Donne. Not long afterwards he was appointed Tuesday lecturer at St. Lawrence Jewry, where his friend, Dr. John Wilkins, was vicar. Pepys visited the church on February 12, 1665, out of curiosity ' to hear the great scholar, Dr. John Wilkins,' but he was more pleased with the fine church than with the sermon. Tillotson's task was to lecture or expound religion. This custom of lecturing had arisen out of the incompetence of parish ministers. A lecturer would deliver his sermon after the service had been read by the minister, for example. The lectureship might be endowed by individuals or a group of individual parishioners, and under Charles the First the Puritans had availed themselves of the privilege. In 1641 an Act of Parliament was passed permitting parishioners to ' set up a lecture and maintain an orthodox minister at their own charges, to preach every Lord's Day where there is no preaching, and to preach one day in the week where there is no lecture.' This week-day was often the local market-day, when a specially good audience could be gathered. After the Restoration the Church employed the privilege, to counteract the Puritans, and Tillotson availed himself of the position to meet the religious needs of London. From this time forward London was his sphere. He held both of these appointments till he became archbishop. Sir John Seeley once hoped for a new race of preachers in the English Church who ' may acquire the power of interesting an audience profoundly, and may make the church once more a place not merely of devotion but also, as all Protestant churches should be, of solid, continuous, and methodical instruction.' This was what a number of able preachers were doing in the second half of the seventeenth century, and none more effectively than Tillotson in his London pulpit. On November 14, 1668, he was chosen to preach the sermon at the consecration of Dr. Wilkins to the bishopric of Chester. Charles, who soon made him a royal chaplain, preferred him to Canterbury, first as prebendary, along with Stillingfleet, and then as dean. There occasionally he preached to congregations which we can see through the lines of a contemporary, John Boyes of Hode Court:

> And first in their formalities are seen
> The learned prebends and the reverend dean.
> The magistrates I next observe, for here
> The purple senate of the town appear.
> Thrice blessed union when the Church and State
> The Word and sword do thus concorporate.
> On t' other side, and to them opposite,
> The gentry have their seats; below in white
> The scholars clad fill their appointed place.
> The multitude crowd in the middle place.

But it was in London that Tillotson addressed his most important audiences: lawyers, politicians, merchants, tradesmen, society people, literary men, young clergymen anxious to learn the art of preaching—in fact, the congregations which at this time made London so throbbing a centre of religious life. Tillotson was one of the great preachers who were adding lustre to the Church in the capital. London was intensely Protestant; men and women of all ranks were also open to instruction, and, in days when no newspapers or magazines competed with the pulpit, the London preachers formed opinion and moulded conduct with unusual efficiency. They were not all Anglicans, but many of them were, including Stillingfleet, Tenison, Patrick, and

Sherlock, and these commended the Anglican theology and practice with wide effect. No small part of the success of this preaching was due to its new vitality. After the Restoration there was a change in the prose of the country. The ornate and elaborate style gave place to one which abjured conceits and rhetorical extravagances, and set itself to be 'concise, clear, succinct, reasonable, prosaic.' As Professor Saintsbury admits, Tillotson 'will rank with Dryden, Halifax, and Temple among the chief introducers of this style in English.' He is less racy than South, but his pulpit style was a revelation to the age of what unadorned, businesslike prose could accomplish in putting religious truth intelligently before the mind of an audience. He did not produce literature, as Dryden, Halifax, and Temple did. When he wrote a sermon, he was about his business, and men felt this in the very style of his speech, plain and direct, driving at the conscience and mind of the congregation. Tillotson practised what he and others in his day asserted : the need of breaking away from the scholastic, academic sermon, with its unliterary masses of quotations and references, and also from the conscious, honeyed rhetoric which had been the pride of preachers like Donne and Jeremy Taylor. Only once, so far as I recollect, did he slip into the florid, false style. Speaking of King William's escape at the battle of the Boyne, he broke out : 'Death came as near to him as was possible without killing him. But the merciful providence of God was pleased to step in for his preservation, almost by a miracle ; for I do not believe that from the first use of great guns to that day any mortal man ever had his shoulder so kindly kissed by a cannon-bullet.' Tillotson and his age as a rule were too seriously interested in religion to care for such flights and fancies of oratory. They had pressing problems, practical and speculative, to engage their attention, particularly the controversies with Romanism, Puritanism, and the ' philosophy ' of Hobbes, and much of Tillotson's strength was devoted to these issues.

It fell to him to engage in controversy, greatly as he disliked the task. When Dr. John Wilkins gave him his step-daughter in marriage, it appears that the lady was unwilling at first for some reason to entertain the proposal. Elizabeth French was a niece of Cromwell, and she may have had views of her own about matrimony. But her guardian overbore her objections with the humorous remark, ' Betty, you shall have him, for he is the best polemical divine this day in England ' ! It is not clear how this could be adduced as a recommendation for a husband, unless the lady was being urged to marry for ambition. But Dr. Wilkins knew his man, at any rate. He could read character, and although Tillotson as yet had done nothing exceptional, his friend anticipated for him a career in the stormy waters of religious debate. His forecast was fulfilled.

Tillotson's primary contest was with atheism,

theoretical and practical. He once mentions ' the ingenious author of a very bad book, I mean *The Leviathan.*' Hobbes was anathema to religious people for various reasons. The main objection taken by Tillotson to his teaching was that it made good and evil relative terms. Hobbes declared that virtue and vice were not grounded in the nature of things, but that ' that is virtue or vice, good or evil, which the supreme authority of a nation declares to be so.' This seemed to Tillotson to leave no place for a moral law which was binding upon the nature of man in virtue of its inherent excellence, and he therefore denounced Hobbes and his principles. Revelation was for Tillotson chiefly the reiteration of the moral law ; he used his great powers in the pulpit to commend this argument. Thus, in publishing some sermons which he had preached and now dedicated to the benchers of Lincoln's Inn, he describes the objects he had had in view : ' First, to shew the unreasonableness of atheism, and of scoffing at religion, which I am sorry to say is so necessary to be done in this age. . . . Secondly, to recommend religion to men from the great and manifold advantages which it brings both to public society and to particular persons. . . . Thirdly, to represent the excellency, more particularly, of the Christian religion, and to vindicate the practice of it from the suspicion of those grievous troubles and difficulties which many imagine it to be attended withal. . . . Fourth, to persuade men to the practice of this holy religion, from the great obligation which the profession of Christianity lays upon men to that purpose, and, more particularly, from the glorious rewards of another life.' Here is a deep and serious design, though it is laid out along lines which are obviously limited.

There were people who still desired polemical preaching of another kind, or prophetical discourses so dear to a certain type of Christian pietism. Tillotson refused to gratify such tastes. Many people, he confesses, ' must be gratified with sublime notions and unintelligible mysteries, with pleasant passages of wit and artificial strains of rhetoric, with nice and unprofitable disputes, with bold interpretations of dark prophecies and peremptory determinations of what will happen next year, and a punctual stating of the time when Antichrist shall be thrown down and Babylon shall fall, and who shall be employed in the work. Or, if their humour lies another way, you must apply yourself to it by making sharp reflections upon matters in present controversy and debate, you must dip your style in gall and vinegar, and be all satire and invective against those that differ from you, and teach people to hate one another and to fall together by the ears ; and this men call gospel-preaching and speaking of seasonable truths.' With all this Tillotson will have no concern. ' If men must needs be gratified with disputes and controversies,' he writes in his best style, ' there are these great controversies between God and the sinner to be stated and determined : whether this be religion, to follow out our own lusts and inclinations, or to endeavour to be like God and to be conformed to him in goodness and mercy and righteousness and truth and faithfulness ?   Whether Jesus Christ be not the Messias and Saviour of the world ? Whether faith and repentance and sincere obedience be not the terms of salvation and the necessary conditions of happiness ?   Whether there shall be a future judgment, when all men shall be sentenc'd according to their works ?   Whether there be heaven and hell ?   Whether good men shall be eternally and unspeakably happy, and wicked men extremely and everlastingly miserable ? These are the great controversies of religion, upon which we are to dispute on God's behalf against sinners.   God asserts, and sinners deny these things, not in words but, which is more emphatical and significant, in their lives and actions.   These are practical controversies of faith, and it concerns every man to be resolved and determined about them, that he may frame his life accordingly.' This conviction made him support any philanthropic or charitable movement which tended to apply religion to life. He incurred odium by favouring the projects of a pioneer of prison-reform and charitable organisation like Thomas Firmin, who was of Socinian and even Unitarian principles. At the Revolution he ardently supported the new religious societies or fellowships which sprang up in the Church to deepen piety and promote the relief of poverty.   These were the practical issues which engaged the sympathy of Tillotson more than any theological wrangles.

In the successful campaign against the Roman Church, which went on for thirty years in England, Tillotson did three things. He made converts from Romanism, he wrote books against it, and he exposed it in his sermons.

His ability in arguing and his persuasive spirit brought individuals out of Romanism. One of these was the young Earl of Shrewsbury, though he was not in time to prevent the deterioration of the youth's character. It was probably his success in this work which made James the Second interfere once. The King was extremely anxious to make a Roman Catholic out of the Earl of Rochester, his Lord Treasurer. Rochester met the royal pressure by demanding that he should hear a debate between chosen champions of the Roman and the Protestant Churches. James had to agree, but he stipulated that there were two Protestants who must not be chosen, Stillingfleet and Tillotson.

When a Romanist attacked Stillingfleet's book on *A Rational Account of the Grounds of the Protestant Religion*, Tillotson replied by publishing *The Rule of Faith*, dedicating it to Stillingfleet himself. This was in 1666. It won for him the degree of D.D. The impression it made upon the thoughtful public may be guessed from a letter of Evelyn to Dr. John Wilkins. ' I have read Dr. Tillotson's *Rule of Faith*, and am obliged to render him thanks for the benefit I acknowledge to have received by it.

Never in my life did I see a thing more illustrated,[1]
more convincing, unless men will be blind because
they will be so.   I am infinitely pleased with his
equal style, dispassionate treatment and Christian
temper to that importunate adversary : for my
part I look upon that business as despatched, and
expect only the grimaces and agonies of dying and
desperate men for the future ; plainly the wound
is mortal.' This work requires to be done over
again, and otherwise. But Evelyn and many
others regarded Tillotson's contribution to the
Roman controversy as a crushing blow.

His preaching on the same theme recalls the
sketch of a grave divine drawn by John Earle,
earlier in the century ; for Tillotson ' in citing of
popish errors, cuts them with arguments, not
cudgels them with barren invectives.'   It was the
one note in his preaching which Charles disliked,
but neither Tillotson nor any other of the Anglican
leaders cared for Charles's idiosyncrasies when it
was a question of religious truth.   Tillotson sometimes clinched his arguments with a cutting word :
as for example in a sermon on the delusion of
purgatory, when he drily observed : ' Bishop Fisher
and several of their own learned writers do frankly
acknowledge that this doctrine of purgatory hath
no sufficient ground in scripture.   Other reasons,
I grant, they have for it, which make them very
loth to quit it ; it is a very profitable doctrine, and
therefore they have taken care to have it more

---

[1] He means, lucid or elucidated.

abundantly confirmed by apparitions of souls from the dead than any other doctrine whatsoever. In short, how little soever they can say for it, it is vain to persuade them to part with it. Demetrius the silversmith argued as well as he could for his goddess Diana from the universal consent of the world in the worship of her : *the great goddess Diana, whom all Asia and the world worshippeth.* But his trusty argument to his workmen was, *Sirs, ye know that by this craft we have our wealth, and this our craft is in danger to be set at nought.*' One of his arguments against transubstantiation, viz. that it was no miracle in the Christian sense of the term, was echoed in an odd quarter during next century. Hume begins his essay on ' Miracles ' by referring to it with praise. ' There is, in Dr. Tillotson's writings, an argument against the real presence, which is as concise and elegant and strong as any argument can possibly be supposed against a doctrine so little worthy of a serious refutation.' But when he preached on such topics, it was not with any academic airs or aim. He was addressing audiences who knew the counter-arguments as practical issues, and he handled them thoroughly with a view to safeguarding Christianity, whether royalty or philosophers were in his audience. There was need for vigilance in all responsible quarters between 1668 and 1678. Mr. Augustine Birrell, in his book on Marvell, notes how these ten years were rendered miserable for him in the House of Commons ' by the passionate conviction that there existed in high quarters of the State a deep, dangerous, and well-considered plot to subvert the Protestant faith and to destroy by armed force Parliamentary Government in England. Marvell was not the victim of a delusion. Such a plot, plan, or purpose undoubtedly existed, though, as it failed, it is now easy to consider the alarm it created to have been exaggerated.' It was this conviction which made Tillotson and his fellow-churchmen speak out, on the religious issue, with frankness of speech. In 1672, for example, he had to preach at Whitehall on ' The Hazard of being Saved in the Church of Rome '; the text was 1 Corinthians iii. 15, ' Saved, yet so as by fire,' and his point was that the Roman Church had built hay, wood, and stubble upon the true foundation. ' I shall present to you some doctrines and practices which have been built upon the foundation of Christianity, to the great hazard and danger of men's salvation. And, to be plain, I mean particularly the Church of Rome. I shall enquire whether our granting a possibility of salvation (tho' with great hazard) to those in the communion of the Roman Church, and their denying it to us, be a reasonable argument and encouragement to any man to betake himself to that Church.' The Duke of York had been surreptitiously betaking himself to the Roman Church ; next year indeed he evaded the Test Act. Tillotson's plain speaking was too much for him, and he never attended the chapel again.

In 1680 Tillotson had quite suddenly to preach at Whitehall. His theme was ' The Protestant

Religion Vindicated from the charge of Singularity and Novelty.' In the course of the sermon he declared that he could not think ' any pretence of conscience warranted any man that is not extraordinarily commissioned as the apostles and first publishers of the gospel were, and cannot justify that commission by miracles as they did, to affront the established religion of a nation (tho' it be false), and openly to draw men off from the established profession of it, in contempt of the magistrate and the law ; all that persons of a different religion can in such a case reasonably pretend to, is to enjoy the private liberty and exercise of their own conscience and religion ; for which they ought to be very thankful, and to forbear the open making of proselytes to their own religion.' Tillotson had safeguarded himself already, but this did sound incautious. Indeed, one lord in the congregation nudged King Charles. ' Sir, sir, do you hear Mr. Hobbes in the pulpit ? ' Tillotson had to print the sermon, and had endless trouble with dissenters and some Anglicans over his words ; indeed, one bishop censured them in the House of Lords. What Tillotson meant, of course, by ' established religion ' was the Protestantism of England ; he was denying the right of the Romanists to practise intrigues and overthrow Protestantism, as they were attempting to do, with the covert approval of Charles. When occasion called for it, he could be outspoken. He could denounce ' the restless and black designs of that sure and inveterate enemy of ours, the

Church of Rome,' but he usually dealt with its
principles and practices gravely. He was neither
narrow nor rhetorical in the controversy. Thus, in
the anxious days of 1688, he told his congregation :
' And now, my brethren, to use the words of St.
Peter, *I testify to you that this is the true grace of
God in which ye stand.* The Protestant reformed
religion, which we in this nation profess, is the very
gospel of Christ, the true ancient Christianity.
And, for God's sake, since in this hour of temptation, when our religion is in so apparent hazard,
we pretend to love it to that degree as to be contented to part with anything for it, let us resolve
to practise it, and to testify our love to it in that
same way that our Saviour would have us show our
love to him, by keeping his commandments.'

Incisive, patient teaching of this kind did its work.
The sermons of men like Tillotson more than coun-
teracted the Romanising policy of the Court. In
fact, during the reign of James the Second ' the
Romish emissaries were hopelessly overmatched.
As Cardinal Howard explained to Burnet, they left
England as boys, grew up abroad, and came back to
preach French and Italian sermons in bad English.
They could not do much against men like Stillingfleet and Tillotson, Sharp and Tenison, Atterbury
and Wake—for the Highest of High Churchmen
were as resolute against Romish doctrine as the
Lowest of the Low.' [1]

[1] Gwatkin, *Church and State in England to the Death of Queen Anne,*
p. 369.

III

Tillotson, however, was too generous and gracious by nature to delight in controversy for controversy's sake. In 1684 he confessed that he hoped for the remainder of his life to be 'released from that irksome and unpleasant work of controversy and wrangling about religion.' Not, he hastens to add, that he had any intention of depreciating the services of sound controversialists. 'If a man have a head clear and cool enough, so as to be master of his own notions and temper in that hot kind of service, he may therein do considerable advantage to the truth.' But he was fifty-four years old, and he wanted the evening of his life to be undisturbed. As things fell out, the last ten years were to be crowded and stormy for him. Charles, under the influence of his mother and sister, had been long negotiating with the Pope and the French king, to change the Anglican Church into a branch of the Roman. But he had no idea of allowing religious considerations to endanger his position ; he was shrewd enough to keep his project a secret, and prudently left the design to his brother. It was a fatal inheritance. James the Second was a stupid, unpopular fanatic, who allowed himself to be led by Jesuit agitators, against the counsels of saner men in his own Church. No sooner had he come to the throne than the French king revoked the Edict of Nantes, feeling that he could afford to do this now that a dull monarch like James was on the English throne. It was disastrous for France, and the refugees who swarmed over to England were an object-lesson to the English Protestants. When Jesuits had political power, who could be safe? The English were roused and alarmed. James, to do him justice, saw how impolitic the step had been, and sought vainly to shift the blame from the Jesuits to Madame de Maintenon and the Archbishop of Paris. The Huguenots were hospitably treated in England, and funds were raised for their support. A prebendary of Canterbury, Dr. Beveridge, objected to reading the Royal Warrant for this collection, as the Huguenots were not Episcopalians. 'Doctor, doctor,' said Tillotson, 'charity is above rubrics.' But the warning was thrown away upon James, who in three short years made England at first uneasy and then resentful under his infatuated policy of Romanising the country.

> From our first Charles by force we wrung our claims.
> Prick'd by the Papal spur, we rear'd,
> We flung the burthen of the second James.

Tennyson often wrote better poetry than that, but he rarely read history better. James imagined that he was in the saddle safely, and he was ignominiously flung off. There is a tale told of him and old Mr. Waller the poet, who was then member of Parliament for Saltash in Cornwall. Waller's daughter was to be married to an English clergyman, and the King sent a sarcastic message to the father, telling him that he wondered how Waller

could marry his daughter ' to a falling church.'
Waller replied, ' The King does me great honour in
taking notice of my domestick affairs ; but I have
lived long enough to observe that this falling church
has got a trick of rising again.' So it had. The
English Church rose, and in rising it upset James.
All parties called for William of Orange to take
over the throne and the Protestant cause. He was
married to Mary, James's eldest daughter, the next
in succession to the throne, and the passion for
religious freedom in England swept James aside in
his favour. Had Protestantism been no more than
a political prejudice, it would not have survived the
Popish plot and the Monmouth rebellion ; these
would have discredited almost any movement that
did not go deeper than the surface of ecclesiastical
opinion and tradition. James in his folly and
fanaticism was blind to the temper of his people;
by the end of 1688 he had scurried off to the Con-
tinent, and the crisis closed with the accession of
William and Mary. Tillotson was only voicing the
mind of Protestant England when he said from the
pulpit : ' Let us humbly beseech Almighty God that
He would long preserve to us the valuable blessing
of our two excellent princes, whom the Providence
of God hath sent among us like two good angels,
not to preserve two or three persons, but almost a
whole nation out of Sodom.'

The relief was great, but the settlement proved
to be unexpectedly difficult. A party in the
Church considered that ' as long as James was

alive, no other persons could be sovereigns of the country ' ; an oath taken to an anointed king as head of the English Church could not be set aside, even though the said monarch was a Roman Catholic and had absconded. This party of the non-jurors held to the superstition that kings were kings by divine right ; they were headed by Arch-bishop Sancroft, and conscientiously clung to their views and places. The Government behaved with patience and forbearance, out of respect for the theoretical scruples of these good men, but obviously it was impossible that bishops and clergy could be allowed to remain in sees and livings and yet be disloyal to the throne. New appointments had to be made, and Tillotson was marked out for pro-motion. Hitherto he had steadily discouraged any proposal to prefer him to the Episcopate. He knew his limitations. Preaching was his real gift. Be-sides, he had had an apoplectic fit in 1687. So for reasons of health and efficiency he was unwilling to change his occupation. When the King desired to make him a bishop, in 1689, he wrote to a friend : ' For the sake of the Protestant religion and their Majesties, for whom I have so true esteem, I would take any business upon me which I am able to stand under ; but I do not love either the ceremony or trouble of a great place. That little good which I have been able to do has been in the city of London, which I foresee will be stripped of its ablest men ; and if I can be serviceable anywhere, it is here.' The King and Queen saw the force of his argument, and he was made Dean of St. Paul's, in succession to Stillingfleet, who became Bishop of Worcester; but something had to be done with the recalcitrant Sancroft, who still clung to Lambeth Palace. Two years exhausted the long patience of the authorities, and he was superseded in 1691 by Tillotson, much to the disgust of Compton, the Bishop of London, who considered that he was entitled to the post. The King and Queen thought otherwise.

It is unhistorical to imagine that the Queen was a partisan of the clerical faction, while the King was no better than a Calvinistic Presbyterian from Holland, who overbore his consort in the matter of ecclesiastical policy. William was a great captain, with interests that went far beyond the internal politics of the Anglican Church. So little did he care for theological Calvinism that he appointed Tillotson and others to high positions, though, like John Hales of Eton, they had ' bade good-night to John Calvin.' William admired Tillotson for deeper reasons. When the Archbishop died, William's remark was, ' I have lost the best friend that I ever had, and the best man that I ever knew.' The Queen was not a whit behind her husband in admiration and affection. When court gossip and scandal among her ladies became intolerable, she used to ask them quietly if they had ever read her favourite sermon, Dr. Tillotson's on Evil Speaking. Honesty and character are valued at a good court, and it was to these qualities that Tillotson owed his promotion, a promotion to which he was most averse.

The new appointments to the Episcopal bench brought some odium on the King and also on the nominees. Yet ' it was only thus that the religious peace could be kept in England against the outcries of the country parsons and the intrigues of the High Church party, which was in that age distinguished, not by ritualistic practices, but by the desire to go back on the Act of Toleration,' [1] a tardy and inadequate measure, but all that William had been able to pass in favour of Protestant dissenters being allowed to worship freely if they took the oath of loyalty. The rigid High Church party loathed dissenters and disliked William's policy of religious freedom. Burnet declares that among many of them ' an inclination to favour dissenters passed for a more heinous thing than leaning to Popery itself.' The hatred felt by such people for Tillotson was neither so vocal nor so vicious as the frenzy of the non-jurors at Sherlock's appointment to succeed him in the Deanery of St. Paul's, but it was thoroughly discreditable. Tillotson to be Archbishop of Canterbury! They waxed bitter over the appointment. He had dared to entertain kindly thoughts of union with dissenters. He had once remarked of the Athanasian Creed, ' I wish we were well rid of it.' He had actually supported a Protestant monarch like William in preference to a Papist head of the Anglican Church like James

[1] G. M. Trevelyan, *England under the Stuarts* (twelfth edition), p. 451.

the Second. His opponents were furious, and a swarm of mean, malicious attacks were made upon his character. Some even went the length of declaring that he had never been baptized! Tillotson behaved with noble magnanimity. He took no notice of the insults, but went on with his work. One day a sealed packet was handed to him, which, on being opened, was found to contain nothing but a mask. He quietly tossed it on the table among his papers. After his death a bundle of papers was discovered in his desk, labelled, ' These are libels ; pray God forgive them ; I do.' There is some satisfaction in the fact that he once felt called to rebuke an offender at this period. In the House of Lords a High Churchman, Sir John Trevor, said aloud in his hearing, ' I hate a fanatic in lawn-sleeves.' The said Sir John had been expelled from the House of Commons for bribery when he was Speaker. Tillotson answered in a low voice, ' And I hate a knave in any sleeves.'

Such was the strife of tongues that raged round the good archbishop as he entered on his high office. It is a relief to turn to his inward life, and to mark how he possessed a city of refuge for the soul. He spent the night before his consecration at Edmonton, praying and fasting. It was Whit-Sunday eve, May 30. In a thanksgiving prayer he blessed God that he had been born ' of honest and religious parents, tho' of a low and obscure condition. I bless Thee that Thou wast pleased to give my ever-honoured and good father the heart to give me, out of the small estate Thou gavest him, so liberal an education, whereby I was put into a capacity to serve Thee. Forgive, I beseech Thee, O Lord, that I have made no better use of the talents and opportunities wherewith Thou hast entrusted me, and accept of that little which by Thy grace I have been enabled sincerely to do for Thee. I bless Thee, O Lord, for the continual and bountiful support of Thy providence, whereby Thou hast also enabled me to return to my parents and their children the kindness I received from them, and to be still a father to them.' Then he added, ' I bless Thee that Thou hast so mercifully and so many times preserved me from the great dangers to which my life was exposed, and from temptations which would have been too hard for me, if Thy grace had not prevented them and kept me from falling into them. This, O Lord, I acknowledge as one of the great blessings of my life, for which I desire continually to magnify Thy great and glorious name. I bless Thee likewise, O Lord, for that measure of health which I have enjoyed, and for my recovery from a great and dangerous sickness, for any happy endowments of mind, for that degree of understanding which Thou hast given me, and for preserving it to me, when my dear mother for so many years of her life lost the use and enjoyment of it, and might have derived that unhappiness to me her child, if Thy merciful goodness had not prevented it. Forgive me, O Lord, that I have made no better use of

the faculties which Thou hast endowed me withal
for Thy glory and the benefit and advantage of
others.' He confessed his sins and shortcomings
in a touching prayer, acknowledging his defects
even in those virtues which his contemporaries
honoured in him. Thus he confesses, ' I have
offended against Thee by anger and impatience
upon many occasions, by neglecting to cultivate
my mind and to govern my passions, by un-
charitableness and evil speaking, and especially
by misspending my precious time, which might
have been employed to excellent purposes. Lord,
what can I say unto Thee for these and innumerable
other provocations of my life ? but there is forgiveness with Thee that Thou mayest be feared. Lord,
let Thy goodness which I have had such plentiful
experience of, lead me to repentance, and not to
be repented of.' It was in such a spirit that Tillotson looked forward to the service of the following
day. ' Since by Thy own wise and good providence,
and the importunate desire of those whom Thou
hast set in authority over us, I am called to the
government and conduct of this miserable, dis-
tracted, and divided Church, in so very difficult and
dangerous a time, be pleased of Thine infinite
mercy and goodness to Thy sinful and most unworthy servant, to afford him the grace and assistance of Thy Holy Spirit to enable him so to discharge the office which Thou hast called him to,
that Thy name may be glorified, and this Church,
which Thou hast committed to his charge, may be

edified in faith and holiness, in love, peace, and union, by his diligence and faithful cares and endeavours ; grant to him such a degree of health, such a vigour of mind, and such a measure of Thy heavenly grace and wisdom as may fit him to be a useful pastor of Thy Church. Give me, O Lord, a mind after Thy own heart, that I may delight to do Thy will, O my God, and let Thy Law be written in my heart. Give me courage and resolution to do my duty, and a heart to spend myself and to be spent in Thy service, and in doing all the good possible I can, the few remaining days of my pilgrimage here on earth.'

His remaining days were few. In November 1691 he and his wife took up residence in Lambeth Palace. Three years later he died there, after a brief, uneventful primacy. The affection and admiration of London came out at his funeral when he was buried in his old church of St. Lawrence Jewry amid extraordinary scenes of public grief.

IV

Tillotson belonged to the Low, or rather to the Broad Church party. It is only a hasty judgment which can pronounce him a rationalist, in the modern sense of the term. He never held that Christianity was a moral philosophy ; it was for him a power of life, though he did not express this in terms either of the Cambridge Platonists or of the evangelical Puritans. There is a tale told of

Selden on his death-bed. He observed to his friend, Archbishop Ussher, that he could not recollect ' any passage out of infinite books and manuscripts he was master of, wherein he could rest his soul, save out of the holy Scriptures, wherein the most remarkable passage that lay upon his spirit was Titus ii. 11-14.' The passage is : *For the grace of God that bringeth salvation hath appeared to all men, teaching us that, denying ungodliness and worldly lusts, we should live soberly, righteously, and godly, in this present world; looking for that blessed hope, and the glorious appearing of the great God and our Saviour Jesus Christ; who gave himself for us, that he might redeem us from all iniquity, and purify unto himself a peculiar people, zealous of good works.* Now this is one of Tillotson's favourite texts. He is constantly quoting from it and applying it. God's grace *teaching* men to *live* a good life, redemption issuing in a zeal for ethical obedience—this was the commanding theme of Tillotson's preaching. Locke did not publish his book on *The Reasonableness of Christianity as Delivered in the Scriptures* until 1695, the year after Tillotson's death, but this title gives the spirit and subject of what Tillotson had taught from the pulpit. Christianity is reasonable religion : it reiterates and supplements the moral law ; reason can discover the moral law, which is natural religion, and verify it in Scripture. And so on. This was indeed the principle of the Cambridge Platonists, who taught that human reason understood both the truths of natural religion (*i.e.* the existence of God, the moral law, future rewards and punishments, and the immortality of the soul) and also the Christian truths so plainly expressed in the Bible. But their religious philosophy included a Divine inspiration in the soul ; the presence of God in the reasoning mind was one of their spiritual dogmas, and with this Tillotson had small sympathy. He would have agreed heartily with Whichcote that ' God is most knowable of anything in the world,' or with John Smith that ' a good man, one that is actuated by religion, lives in constant converse with his reason ' ; but his mind did not respond to the mystical instincts and intuitions in the religious philosophy of his friends. To a man of his temperament the passions and affections seemed hopelessly overworked as the basis for religion, and he eschewed them in favour of more deliberate and conscious arguments.

Hence there is a lack of the heroic note in Tillotson's ethic. It tends to be prudential and utilitarian rather than a challenge to sacrifice and to the self-surrender which counts not the cost if the cause can be served. Tillotson, in his eagerness to prove that Christianity is not opposed to the interests of men, has to explain away some of the severer elements in the New Testament, and if he must admit that there are difficulties in Christianity, he pleads that at least they are not greater than those we meet in the ordinary pursuits of life. Does the Bible say that we must enter into the kingdom of God through many tribulations, or that whoever will live godly in Christ Jesus must suffer persecution? Yes, but such sayings 'are not equally to be extended to all places and times.' They are specially meant for a definite historical period, 'when the Providence of God thought fit to establish the Christian religion upon the innocent lives and patient sufferings' of the primitive Christians. This recognition of a purely historical element in such references is not unjust. But, in Tillotson's hands, it involves a reduced Christianity all round, for he has to explain in the same way that some of the characteristic promises possess merely a relative significance. Take texts like these: *All things whatsoever ye desire when ye pray, believe that ye receive them, and ye shall have them.—If ye shall ask anything in my name, I will do it.—If ye abide in me and my words abide in you, ye shall ask what ye will, and it shall be done unto you.* 'These promises,' says Tillotson, 'I take to contain something extraordinary and peculiar to the first times of Christianity.' He believes that the aid of God's Spirit is still needful, but 'it is not reasonable to expect the same extraordinary operation of the Spirit of God upon the minds of men which we read of in the first beginning of Christianity.' Again he is feeling for a truth, and yet this is where the common-sense theology of Tillotson and his school handicapped itself, as it reacted against the pietistic extravagances of the period. Still, there is no doubt that in preaching thus he appealed successfully to his generation, many of whom were thankful to find Christianity cleared from the ecstatic and riotous sentiment of the sects, from mystical rhapsodies as well as from scholastic controversies. The vindication of reason as a divine faculty was hailed with sincere relief. ' The vigour of English theology at this period—and it was the golden period of English theology—is due to the fact that, for the time, reason and Christian theology were in spontaneous alliance.' [1] Sir Leslie Stephen is correct in this verdict, and correct in stressing the term ' spontaneous,' for the reasoning of these theologians and preachers was a vital impulse, not an afterthought born of apologetic straits. But it is less adequate to explain Tillotson's popularity as the mere result of his merit ' of expressing fully the vein of thought most characteristic of his later contemporaries.' There have been writers whose power lay in their capacity for voicing what others were thinking around them. There have been preachers who enjoyed fame which was largely due to their skill in reproducing some current philosophising of the schools. Even this has its function. When some of Voltaire's opponents sneered at him for being the first man in the world to write down what his contemporaries were thinking, they were deriding a remarkable gift of divination, even if Voltaire's genius had included little more—and it included much more. Any one who has the gift of expressing forcibly what his contemporaries are feeling in some dumb way, renders a service to his

[1] *English Thought in the Eighteenth Century*, vol. i. p. 79.

time. If he does it with conviction, and also with
freshness, he makes articulate the vague emotions
that otherwise might fail to find expression, and
thus remain less powerful as influences for good.
It was part of Tillotson's service to seventeenth-
century England that he stated from the pulpit
a number of diffused ideas about religion and reason
which had been growing in the minds of ordinary
people. His statement reinforced their hold upon
the age. And in the particular matter of setting
forth Christianity as a claim on ethical obedience
and intelligent opinion he was not playing the
rôle of an acute apologist who feels that he must
say something intellectual on behalf of his creed.
Tillotson's defence is an attack ; it is the instinc-
tive movement of a living mind in religion. The
limitations of his argument, and the dangerous
consequences of some theses he advanced, are to-
day obvious. Indeed, they became obvious in the
next century, when a rationalist like Collins could
call him one ' whom all English freethinkers hail
as their head.' But in the day when he wrote, his
tenacious statement of reasonable Christianity was
timely and trenchant. His excellence lay in seeing
that this involved moral requirements as well as
mental. So keenly did he feel this, that he had a
frank antipathy to anything like ' enthusiasm.'
In those days ' enthusiasm ' was equivalent to
what we now call ' fanaticism.' Like Locke and
other leaders of thought, Tillotson objected to it
not only because it defied or denied reason, but

because it often made light of moral standards. Locke meant by it 'the various ravings men have embraced for religion,' and Tillotson included in it the views of all who claimed a direct inspiration which ignored the conscience and the mind, such views as were held by Ranters, Anabaptists, and votaries of the inner light, the fanatics whom Baxter knew as 'the Sectaries and Seekers, Quakers, Behmenists, etc.' He detested 'those luscious doctrines of the antinomians,' which vexed men like Bunyan, Baxter, and George Fox. Some of his most permanent teaching is contained in the arguments he brings forward so bluntly against that heresy. But then his emphasis upon the moral quality of religion led him to underrate anything like a disinterested love of virtue ; he actually seems to have considered that such love, devoid of any prospect of reward or fear of punishment, was no better than a dry speculation, which would end, as it did with the Sadducees, in 'giving over all serious pursuit of religion.' Hence the tone of passages such as those I have cited under 'Zeal not according to Knowledge.'

He wrote some treatises, he edited the post-humous works of Dr. Wilkins and Dr. Barrow, and he read over the historical manuscript of Burnet. But the literature he produced was the literature of sermons, which ranged far and wide over the interests of practical religious Englishmen. He preached on a variety of topics, not only upon ' The wisdom of being religious ' and ' The advantages of religion,' but on 'The true remedy against the troubles of life' (four sermons), 'The sin and danger of adding to the doctrine of the gospel,' 'The deceitfulness and danger of sin,' 'The necessity of the knowledge of the holy Scriptures,' 'The Christian life a life of faith,' 'The life of Jesus Christ considered as our example' (three sermons on this), and 'The necessity of supernatural grace, in order to a Christian life.' He would preach long sermons on dogma, on Christian evidences, on the attributes of God, and the immortality of the soul ; but also he would expound the parables of Jesus and handle themes like 'True liberty the result of Christianity,' or 'The care of our souls, the one thing needful.' He dipped into details. He could direct his congregation to provide children with proper prayers, as well as preach on 'The love of God to man, in the Incarnation of Christ.' He could be startlingly definite in social ethics, as we shall see, even arguing at length why mothers should nurse their children. And he could preach exhaustively on the Atonement as a satisfaction to the Divine justice, for Tillotson was orthodox on the Atonement, although it is perhaps true to add that he did not so much preach it as preach about it. The passages I have chosen from his sermons will show the scope and alertness of his mind, and also the ethical glow which pervaded his preaching. Only those who have not read the sermons, or who have forgotten what they read, could speak of them as 'frigid moral essays.' They are not that, even to our modern taste, which demands very different fare, and they were not considered commonplace by the congregations who listened eagerly to them. Frigid moral essays are not translated into French and German and Dutch, as Tillotson's sermons were. He is one of the few English preachers who have won a Continental reputation. And in his own country his fame lasted far into the eighteenth century, whose thought he anticipated in more ways than one. The copyright of his discourses brought ten thousand five hundred guineas to his widow — a telling proof of their value even from a monetary point of view. Addison and Steele honoured him highly. Dryden generously said that if he had any talent for English prose, he owed it to the fact that he had often read the writings of ' the great Archbishop Tillotson,' and there is no need to whittle away Dryden's praise. Even later, when new voices had arisen in the pulpit of England, he was not soon forgotten. Boswell was once persuaded to ask Johnson what were the best English sermons in point of style. ' Tillotson's ? ' said Boswell, by way of an opening. ' Why, not now,' Johnson answered ; ' I should not advise a young preacher at this day to imitate Tillotson's style ; though, I don't know. I should be cautious of objecting to what has been applauded by so many suffrages.'

I have made this book of selections, to show that these ' suffrages ' were not unjustified. The passages have been chosen, either because they are characteristic of Tillotson, or because they seem to possess some permanent claim to notice in a day when the problems of reason in religion, of true Catholicism, of Christianity as an ethical force, and of ecclesiastical readjustment, have come up again, in forms not wholly different from those of Tillotson's period. I have used the folio edition in three volumes ; it is inaccurately printed, and, with modern popular readers in view, I have not followed the archaic spelling and punctuation invariably.

However, write as he may, a man is best known by his devotions. The prayer used by Tillotson as he began to write his sermons shows the seriousness and candour of his faith, and these selections are best read in the light of it.

' O Lord God of truth, I humbly beseech Thee to enlighten my mind by Thy Holy Spirit, that I may discern the true way to eternal salvation, and to free me from all prejudice and passion, from every corrupt affection and interest that may either blind me or seduce me in my search after it. Make me impartial in my enquiry after truth, and ready, whenever it is delivered to me, to receive it in the love of it, to obey it from the heart, to practise it in my life, and to continue stedfast in the profession of it to the end of my days.

' I perfectly resign myself, O Lord, to Thy conduct and direction, in confidence that Thy mercy and goodness is such that Thou wilt not suffer those who sincerely desire to know the truth and rely upon Thy guidance, finally to miscarry. And if in anything which concerns the true worship and service of Thee, my God, and the everlasting happiness of my soul, I am in any error and mistake, I earnestly beg of Thee to convince me of it and to lead me into the way of truth, and to confirm and establish me in it daily more and more.

' And I beseech Thee, O Lord, always to preserve in me a great compassion and sincere charity towards those that are in error and ignorance of Thy truth, beseeching Thee to take pity on them and to bring them to the knowledge of it that they may be saved.

' And because our blessed Saviour hath promised that all who do His will shall know His doctrine, grant, O Lord, that I may never knowingly offend Thee in anything or neglect to do what I know to be Thy will and my duty.

' Grant, O heavenly Father, these my humble and hearty requests, for His sake Who is the Way, the Truth, and the Life, my blessed Saviour and Redeemer Jesus Christ. Amen.'

DATES

1630 : born in the parish of Halifax.

        1633-1645 : Laud archbishop of Canterbury.

        1642-1649 : Civil War.

1647 : enters Cambridge University.

1651 : Fellow of Clare College.

        1653-1658 : Cromwell Protector.

1656 : in London.

1660 : ordained by Bishop Sydserf.

        1660-1685 : Charles the Second.

1661 : curate at Cheshunt, Hertfordshire.

        1662 : The Act of Uniformity.

1663 : rector of Kedington, Suffolk.

preacher at Lincoln's Inn.

1664 : lecturer at St. Lawrence Jewry.

married to Elizabeth French.

1666 : degree of D.D.

1669 : royal chaplain.

prebendary of Canterbury.

1672 : dean of Canterbury.

1675 : prebendary of St. Paul's.

        1685 : Accession of James the Second.

        1689 : William and Mary.

1689 : dean of St. Paul's.

1691 : archbishop of Canterbury.

1694 : died, November 22.

SELECTIONS

I. DISCUSSIONS AND ARGUMENTS

AGAINST EVIL-SPEAKING [1]

GENERAL persuasives to repentance and a good life, and invectives against sin and wickedness at large, are certainly of good use to recommend religion and virtue, and to expose the deformity and danger of a vicious course. But it must be acknowledged, on the other hand, that these general discourses do not so immediately tend to reform the lives of men, because they fall among the crowd, but do not touch the conscience of particular persons in so sensible and awakening a manner as when we treat of particular duties and sins, and endeavour to put men upon the practice of the one and to reclaim them from the other, by proper arguments taken from the Word of God and from the nature of particular virtues and vices. . . . And to this end I have pitched upon one of the common and reigning vices of the age, calumny and evil-speaking, by which men contract so much guilt to themselves and create so much trouble to others,

[1] The text of this famous sermon, preached before the King and Queen at Whitehall on February 25, 1694, is Titus iii. 2 : *speak evil of no man.*

and from which, it is to be feared, few or none are wholly free.

I. This vice consists in saying things of others which tend to their disparagement and reproach, to the taking away or lessening of their reputation and good name. And this, whether the things said be true or not. If they be false and we know it, then it is downright calumny; and if we do not know it, but take it upon the report of others, it is however a slander, and so much the more injurious because really groundless and undeserved. If the thing be true, and we know it to be so, yet it is a defamation, and tends to the prejudice of our neighbour's reputation. And it is a fault to say the evil of others which is true, unless there be some good reason for it. Besides, it is contrary to that charity and goodness which Christianity recognises, to divulge the faults of others, though they be really guilty of them, without necessity or some very good reason for it.

Again, it is evil-speaking and the vice condemned in the text, whether we be the first authors of the report or relate it from others, because the man that is evil spoken of is equally defamed either way.

Again, whether we speak evil of a man to his face or behind his back. The former may indeed seem to be the more generous, but yet is a great fault, and that which we call *reviling*; the latter is more mean and base, and that which we properly call *slander* or *backbiting*.

And lastly, whether it be done directly and in express terms, or more obscurely and by way of oblique insinuation, whether by way of downright reproach or with some crafty preface of commendation; for, so it have the effect to defame, the manner of address does not much alter the case; the one may be the more dexterous but is not one jot less faulty. For many times the deepest wounds are given by these smoother and more artificial ways of slander, as by asking questions—' Have you not heard so and so of such a man? I say no more. I only ask the question '—or by general intimations that ' they are loth to say what they have heard of such a one, are very sorry for it, and do not at all believe it ' (if you will believe them) —and this many times without telling the thing, but leaving you in the dark to suspect the worst.

II. We will now consider the extent of this prohibition, *to speak evil of no man*, and the due bounds and limitations of it. For it is not to be understood absolutely to forbid us to say anything concerning others that is bad. This in some cases may be necessary and our duty, and in several cases very fit and reasonable. . . .

It is not only lawful but very commendable and many times our duty to do this in order to the probable amendment of the person of whom evil is spoken. In such a case we may tell a man of his faults privately, or, when it may not be fit for us to use that boldness and freedom, we may reveal his faults to one that is more fit and proper to reprove him and will probably make no other use of this discovery but in order to his amendment. And this is so far from being a breach of charity that it is one of the best testimonies of it. For perhaps the party may not be guilty of what hath been reported of him, and then it is a kindness to give him the opportunity of vindicating himself. Or, if he be guilty, perhaps being privately and prudently told of it he may repent. . . . But then we must take care that this be done out of kindness, and that nothing of our own passion be mingled with it, and that, under pretence of reproving and reforming men, we do not reproach and revile them, and tell them of their faults in such a manner as if we did it to show our authority rather than our charity. It requires a great deal of address and gentle application so to manage the business of reproof as not to irritate and exasperate the person whom we reprove, instead of curing him.

This likewise is not only lawful but our duty, when we are legally called to bear witness concerning the faults and crime of another. A good man would not be an accuser, unless the public good or the prevention of some great evil should require it. And then the plain reason of the thing will sufficiently justify a voluntary accusation ; otherwise it hath always among well-mannered people been esteemed very odious for a man to be officious in this kind and a forward informer concerning the misdemeanours of others. But when a man is called to give testimony in this kind, in obedience to the laws, and out of reverence to the oaths taken, in such cases he is so far free from deserving blame for so doing, that it would be an unpardonable fault in him to conceal the truth or any part of it.

It is lawful to publish the faults of others in our own necessary defence and vindication. When a man cannot conceal another's faults without betraying his own innocency, no charity requires a man to suffer himself to be defamed, to save the reputation of another man. . . .

This also is lawful for caution and warning to a third person, that is in danger to be infected by the company or the example of another, or may be greatly prejudiced by reposing too much confidence in him, having no knowledge or suspicion of his bad qualities. But even in this case we ought to take great care that the ill character we give of any man may be spread no further than is necessary to the good end we designed in it.

Besides these more obvious and remarkable

cases, this prohibition doth not, I think, hinder but that in ordinary conversation men may mention that ill of others which is already made as public as it well can be, or that one friend may not in freedom speak to another of the miscarriage of a third person, where he is secure no ill use will be made of it, and that it will go no further to his prejudice, provided always that we take no delight in hearing or speaking ill of others. And the less we do it, though without any malice or design of harm, still the better, because this shows that we do not feed upon ill reports and take pleasure in them.

These are all the usual cases in which it may be necessary for us to speak evil of other men. And these are so evidently reasonable that the prohibition in the text cannot with reason be extended to them. And if no man would allow himself to say anything to the prejudice of another man's good name but in these and the like cases, the tongues of men would be very innocent and the world would be very quiet.

III. I proceed in the third place to consider the evil of this practice, both in the causes and the consequences of it. . . .

One of the deepest and most common causes of evil-speaking is ill-nature and cruelty of disposition. Men do commonly incline to the cen-

sorious and uncharitable side. . . . To speak evil
of others is almost become the general entertain-
ment of all companies, and the great and serious
business of most meetings and visits, after the
necessary ceremonies and compliments are over, is
to sit down and backbite all the world. 'Tis the
sauce of conversation, and all discourse is counted
but flat and dull which hath not something of
piquancy and sharpness in it against somebody.

But especially if it concerns one of another party,
and that differs from us in matters of religion ; in
this case all parties seem to be agreed that they do
God good service in blasting the reputation of their
adversaries. And though they all pretend to be
Christians and the disciples of him who taught
nothing but kindness and meekness and charity,
yet it is strange to see with what a savage and
murderous disposition they will fly at one another's
reputation and tear it in pieces. . . . To speak
impartially, the zealots of all parties have got a
scurvy trick of lying for the truth. . . .

Another cause of the commonness of this vice is
that many are so bad themselves in one kind or
other. For to think and speak ill of others is not
only a bad thing but a sign of a bad man. When
men are bad themselves, they are glad of any
opportunity to censure others, and are always apt
to suspect that evil of other men which they know

by [1] themselves. They cannot have a good opinion of themselves, and therefore are very unwilling to have so of anybody else. And for this reason they endeavour to bring men to a level, hoping it will be some justification of them if they can but render others as bad as themselves.

Another source of this vice is malice and revenge. When men are in heat and passion, they do not consider what is true but what is spiteful and mischievous, and speak evil of others in revenge of some injury which they have received from them ; and when they are blinded by their passions, they lay about them madly and at a venture, not much caring whether the evil they speak be true or not. Nay, many are so devilish as to invent and raise false reports on purpose to blast men's reputations. . . .

Another cause of evil-speaking is envy. Men look with an evil eye upon the good that is in others. This makes them greedy to entertain and industriously to publish anything that may serve to that purpose, thereby to raise themselves upon the ruins of other men's reputations. And therefore, as soon as they have got an ill report of any good man by the end, to work they presently go, to send it abroad by the first post. For the string is always ready

---

[1] *i.e.* about or against. The same usage occurs in the A.V. of 1 Corinthians iv. 4 : ' For I know nothing by myself.'

upon their bow to let fly this arrow with an incredible swiftness through city and country, for fear the innocent man's justification should overtake it.

Another cause of evil-speaking is impertinence and curiosity, an itch of talking and meddling in the affairs of other men which do nowise concern them. Some persons love to mingle themselves in all business, and are loth to seem ignorant of so important a piece of news as the faults and follies of men, or any bad thing that is talked of in good company. And therefore they do with great care pick up ill stories as good matter of discourse in the next company that is worthy of them. And this, perhaps, not out of any great malice but for want of something better to talk of. . . .

I proceed to consider the ordinary but very pernicious consequences and effects of it, both to others and to ourselves. First to others, the parties I mean that are slandered. To them it is certainly a great injury, and commonly a high provocation, but always matter of no small grief and trouble. . . . Secondly, the consequences of this vice are as bad or worse to ourselves. Whoever is wont to speak evil of others gives a bad character of himself even to those whom he desires to please, who, if they be wise enough, will conclude that he speaks of them to others as he does of others to them. . . .

IV. I proceed in the fourth place to add some arguments and considerations to take men off from this vice. . . .

Consider how cheap a kindness it is to speak well—at least, not to speak ill of any. A good word is an easy obligation, but not to speak ill requires only our silence, which costs us nothing. Some instances of charity are chargeable, as to relieve the wants and necessities of others ; the expense deters many from this kind of charity. But, were a man never so covetous, he might afford another man his good word ; at least he might refrain from speaking ill of him, especially if it be considered how dear many have paid for a slanderous and reproachful word. . . .

Consider that no quality doth ordinarily recommend one more to the favour and goodwill of men than to be free from this vice. Every one desires such a man's friendship and is apt to repose a great trust and confidence in him. . . .

When ye are going to speak reproachfully of others, consider whether ye do not lie open to just reproach in the same or some other kind. There are very few so innocent and free either from infirmities or greater faults as not to be obnoxious to reproach upon one account or other ; even the wisest and most virtuous and most perfect among men have some little vanity or affectation which

lays them open to the raillery of a mimical [1] and
malicious wit.   Therefore we should often turn our
thoughts upon ourselves and look into that part
of the wallet which men commonly fling over their
shoulders and keep behind them, that they may not
see their own faults.   And when we have searched
that well, let us remember our Saviour's rule, *He
that is without sin, let him first cast the stone. . . .*

V. I shall in the last place give some rules and
directions for the prevention and cure of this great
evil among men.

Never say any evil of any man but what you
certainly know.   Whenever you positively accuse
and indite any man of any crime, though it be in
private and among friends, speak as if you were
upon your oath, because God sees and hears you.
. . . Never speak evil of any man upon common
fame, which for the most part is false but almost
always uncertain whether it be true or not.   Not
but that it is a fault in most cases to report the evil
of men which is true, and which we certainly know
to be so ; but if I cannot prevail to make men
wholly to abstain from this fault, I would be glad
to compound with some persons to gain this point
of them, however, because it will retrench nine
parts in ten of evil-speaking in the world.

---

[1] *i.e.* characteristic of a ' mimic,' who excites laughter by a ludicrous
mimicry of some one or something.

Before you speak evil of any man, consider whether he hath not obliged you by some real kindness; and then it is a bad return to speak ill of him who has done us good. Consider also whether you may not come hereafter to be acquainted with him, related to him, or obliged by him whom you have thus injured. And how will you then be ashamed when you reflect upon it, and perhaps have reason also to believe that he to whom you have done this injury is not ignorant of it. . . .

Let us accustom ourselves to pity the faults of men and to be truly sorry for them; and then we shall take no pleasure in publishing them. He is not a good Christian who is not heartily sorry for the faults even of his greatest enemies. And if he will be so, he will discover [lay bare] them no further than is necessary to some good end.

Whenever we hear any man evil-spoken of, if we know any good of him, let us say that. It is always the more human and the more honourable part to stand up in defence and vindication of others than to accuse and bespatter them. Possibly the good you have heard of them may not be true; but it is much more probable that the evil which you have heard of them is not true neither. . . .

That you may not speak ill of any, do not delight to hear ill of them. Give no countenance to busybodies and those who love to talk of other men's faults. Or, if you cannot decently reprove them because of their quality, then divert the discourse some other way. Or, if you cannot do that, by seeming not to mind it you may sufficiently signify that you do not like it.

Let every man mind himself and his own duty and concernment. Do but endeavour in good earnest to mend thyself, and it will be work enough for one man, and leave thee but little time to talk of others. . . .

Lastly, let us set a watch before the door of our lips, and not speak but upon consideration—I do not mean to speak finely, but fitly. Especially when thou speakest of others, consider of whom and what thou art going to speak. Use great caution and circumspection in this matter; look well about thee, on every side of the thing and on every person in the company, before thy words slip from thee, which, when they are once out of thy lips, are for ever out of thy power. . . . If we have a mind wise enough and good enough, we may easily find a field large enough for innocent conversation, such as will harm nobody and yet be acceptable enough to the better and wiser part of mankind. . . .

All that now remains is to reflect upon what hath been said, and to urge you and myself to do accordingly.   For all is nothing, if we do not practise what we so plainly see to be our duty.   Many are so taken up with the deep points and mysteries of religion that they never think of the common duties and offices of human life.   But faith and a good life are so far from clashing with one another that the Christian religion hath made them inseparable.   True faith is necessary to a good life, and a good life is the genuine product of a right belief ; and therefore the one ought never to be pressed to the prejudice of the other.

I foresee what will be said, because I have heard it so often said in the like case, that there is not a word of Jesus Christ in all this.   No more is there in the text.   And yet I hope that Jesus Christ is truly preached whenever his will and laws and the duties enjoined by the Christian religion are inculcated upon us.—[i. 394-404.]

ATHEISM

AT the first planting of the Christian religion in the world, God was pleased to accompany it with a miraculous power.   But after it was planted, this miraculous power ceased, and God hath now left it to be maintained and supported by more ordinary and human ways, by the countenance of authority and assistance of laws, which were never more necessary than in this degenerate age, which is prodigiously sunk into atheism and profaneness and is running headlong into a humour of scoffing at God and religion and everything that is sacred. For some ages before the Reformation atheism was confined to Italy, and had its chief residence at Rome. All the mention that is of it in the history of those times the Papists themselves give us in the lives of their own popes and cardinals, excepting two or three small philosophers that were retainers to that court. So that this atheistical humour among Christians was the spawn of the gross superstitions and corrupt manners of the Romish church and court. And indeed nothing is more natural than for extremes in religion to beget one another, like the vibrations of a pendulum which, the more violently you swing it one way, the farther it will return the other. But in the last age atheism travelled over the Alps and infected France, and now of late it hath crossed the seas and invaded our nation, and hath prevailed to amazement;[1] for I do not think that there are any people in the world that are

---

[1] To refute ' atheism '—though the term was used loosely—was quite a practical problem in the seventeenth century for English moralists and divines, as may be seen in the pages of Bunyan and Baxter as well as of Henry More and Cudworth. Scott describes an ugly specimen of atheist in Bletson, the Commonwealth official who comes into *Woodstock*.

generally more indisposed to it and can worse brook it, seriousness and zeal in religion being almost the natural temper of the English. So that nothing is to me matter of greater wonder than that in a grave and sober nation profaneness should ever come to gain so much ground, and the best and wisest religion in the world to be made the scorn of fools. For, besides the profane and atheistical discourses about God and religion, and senseless abuses of this sacred Book (the great instrument of our salvation) which are so frequent in the public places of resort—I say, besides these (I speak it knowingly), a man can hardly pass the streets without having his ears grated and pierced with such horrid and blasphemous oaths and curses as are enough, if we were guilty of no other sin, to sink a nation.—[i. 39.]

HOW BAD MEN DIE

IT cannot be denied but that some very bad men (as bad as we can well imagine) have passed out of this world not only quiet and undisturbed, but with a great deal of courage and resolution. But this, when it happens, may probably enough be ascribed to one or more of these causes. Either to the mistake of the bystanders,

who take silence for peace, and because a man is
of a strong resolution and hath good command of
himself and does not think fit to trouble others in
a matter in which he thinks they can give him no
comfort and relief, they interpret this to be tran-
quillity of mind. Because he holds his peace and
says nothing, they think he hath peace and that
all is quiet within. But I remember the observation of a very wise historian, Phil. Comines,[1] who
says that he knew in his time several great persons
who in ordinary conversation and to a superficial
view seemed to be very happy and contented, but
yet to them that knew them more intimately, and
in their private freedoms and recesses, were the
most miserable and discontented persons in the
world. This I confess is very rare, for men to
conceal a great trouble, and more yet for a man to
dissemble when dying ; and yet there is reason to
believe it sometimes happens. Sometimes the death
of a very bad man proceeds from stupidity and
want of a just sense of the danger of his condition,
and this from want of discipline and instruction in
the nature and principles of religion. This temper
looks like courage, because it is fearlessness of
danger ; but this fearlessness is founded in great

[1] Philip de Comines, the diplomatist, who has been called the Tacitus
of France. His *Mémoires*, written between 1488 and 1495, were published in 1509.

ignorance and want of apprehension, whereas a true courage discerns the danger and yet thinks it fit and reasonable to venture upon it. Now, this stupidity of dying men who have lived very ill is commonly the case of such as have been brought up in great ignorance and have lived in great sensuality, by which means their spirits are immersed and even stifled in carnality and sense; and no wonder if they who live like beasts die after the same manner.[1]—[iii. 197, 198.]

The common custom is (and I fear it is too common), when the physician has given over his patient, then and not till then to send for the minister, not so much to inquire into the man's condition and to give him suitable advice as to minister comfort and to speak peace to him at a venture. But let me tell you that herein you put an extremely difficult task upon us, in expecting that we should pour wine and oil into the wound before it be searched, and speak smooth and comfortable things to a man that is but just brought to a sense of the long course of a lewd and wicked life impenitently continued in. Alas! what comfort can we give to men in such a case? We are

---

[1] This subject preoccupied the mind of many leading writers even in the eighteenth century; Addison has a paper on it in *The Spectator* (n. 289). But Byron's rough sentence had a truth in it: 'a death-bed is a matter of nerves and constitution, and not of religion.'

loth to drive them to despair, and yet we must not destroy them by presumption ; pity and good nature do strongly tempt us to make the best of their case and to give them all the little hopes which with any kind of reason we can—and God knows it is but very little that we can give to such persons upon good ground, for it all depends upon the degree and sincerity of their repentance, which God only knows and we can but guess at.—[i. 29, 30.]

PRIVATE BAPTISM

I KNOW that of late years, since our unhappy confusions, this sacrament hath been very frequently administered in private, and ministers have been, in a manner, and to avoid the great mischief of separation, necessitated to comply with the obstinacy of the greater and more powerful of their parishioners, who for their ease or humour, or for the convenience of a pompous christening, will have their children baptized at home by their minister, or, if he refuse, will get some other minister to do it—which is very irregular. Now I would entreat such persons calmly to consider how contrary to reason and to the plain design of the institution of this sacrament, this perverse custom and their obstinate resolution in it is.

For is there any civil society or corporation into which persons are admitted without some kind of solemnity ? And is the privilege of being admitted members of the Christian Church and heirs of the great and glorious promises and blessings of the new covenant of the gospel less considerable and fit to be conferred with less solemnity ?—[i. 490, 491.]

WHO ARE OUR 'BETTERS'?

OUR blessed Lord, when he was upon earth, did in nothing show himself more like the Son of God than in going about *doing good*. And the wonderful works which he did give testimony of his divinity, not so much as they were acts of power as of goodness, and wrought for the benefit and advantage of men. And the true advantage of greatness and wealth and power does not consist in this, that it sets men above others, but that it puts them in a capacity of doing more good than others. Men are apt to call them their ' betters,' who are higher and richer than themselves ; but in a true and just esteem of things they only are our ' betters ' who do more good than we. From the meanest creature below us up to God himself, they are the best and happiest and most perfect beings who are the most useful and beneficial to others, who have the most power and the strongest inclinations to do good.—[iii. 374.]

HOW IS THE BIBLE INSPIRED ?

IF any one enquire further, how far the pen-men of Scripture were inspired in the writing of these books, whether only so far as to be secured from mistake in the delivery of any message or doctrine from God, or in the relation of any history or matter of fact, yet so as they were left every man to his own style and manner of expression, or that every thing they wrote was immediately dictated to them, and that, not only the sense of it but the very words and phrases by which they express things, and that they were merely instruments or pen-men—I shall not take upon me to determine ; I shall only say this in general, that, considering the end of this inspiration,[1] which was to inform the world certainly of the mind and will of God,

---

[1] Dr. John Goodwin, Tillotson's learned contemporary, in a tract on *The Divine Authority of the Scriptures*, maintained that ' the true and proper foundation of the Christian religion is not ink and paper, not any book or books, not any writing or writings whatsoever, whether translations or originals, but that substance of matter, those glorious counsels of God concerning the salvation of the world by Jesus Christ, which are indeed represented and declared both in the translations and originals, but are distinct from both.'

it is necessary for every man to believe that the inspired pen-men of Scripture were so far assisted as was necessary to this end ; and he that thinks upon good grounds that this end cannot be secured unless every word and syllable were immediately dictated, he hath reason to believe it so ; but if any man upon good grounds thinks that the end of writing the Scripture may be sufficiently secured without that, he hath no reason to conclude that God, who is not wanting in what is necessary, is guilty of doing what is superfluous. . . . We find that the evangelists, in relating the discourses of Christ, are very far from agreeing in the particular expressions and words, though they do agree in the substance of the discourses ; but if the words had been dictated by the Spirit of God, they must have agreed in them. For when St. Luke differs from St. Matthew in relating what our Saviour said, it is impossible that they should both relate it right as to the very words and forms of expression ; but they both relate the substance of what he said. And if it had been of concernment that every-thing they wrote should be dictated *ad apicem*, to a tittle, by the Spirit of God, it is of the same concernment still that the providence of God should have secured the Scriptures since, to a tittle, from the least alteration. Which, that it is not done, appears by the various readings [1] both of the Old and New Testament, concerning which no man can infallibly say that this is right and not the other. It seems sufficient in this matter to assert that the Spirit of God did reveal to the pen-men of the Scriptures what was necessary to be revealed, and, as to all other things, that he did superintend them in the writing of it, so far as to secure them from any material error or mistake in what they have delivered.—[iii. 428, 429.]

THE BIBLE A PLAIN BOOK

IT is not necessary that a rule should be so plain that we should perfectly understand it at first sight; it is sufficient if it be so plain that those of better capacity and understanding may, with due diligence and application of mind, come to the true knowledge of it, and those of a lower and more ordinary capacity, by the help and instruction of a teacher. Euclid's Elements is a book sufficiently plain to teach a man geometry, but yet not so plain that any man at first reading should understand it perfectly; but by diligent

---

[1] These had been forced upon the notice of seventeenth-century England, much to the disgust of Puritans like John Owen, by the publication of Brian Walton's massive *Polyglott Bible* in 1654-1657.

reading, by a due application and steady attention of mind, a man of extraordinary sagacity and understanding may come to understand the principles and demonstrations of it, and those of more ordinary capacity, with the help of a teacher, may come to the knowledge of it. So when we say that the Scriptures are plain in all things necessary to faith and a good life, we do not mean that every man at first hearing or reading of these things in it shall perfectly understand them ; but by diligent reading and consideration, if he be of good apprehension and capacity, he may come to a sufficient knowledge of them, and if he be of meaner capacity, and be willing to learn, he may, by the help of a teacher, be brought to understand them without any great pains. And such teachers God hath appointed in his Church for this very purpose, and a succession of them to continue to the end of the world.

In a word, when we say the Scriptures are plain to all capacities in all things necessary, we mean that any man of ordinary capacity, by his own diligence and care, in conjunction with the helps and advantages which God hath appointed, and in the due use of them, may attain to the knowledge of everything necessary to his salvation ; and that there is no book in the world more plain and better fitted to teach a man any art or science than the Bible is to direct and instruct men in the way to heaven.—[ii. 213, 214.]

Those doctrines of religion and those interpretations of Scripture have ever been to me the most suspected which need abundance of wit and a great many criticisms to make them out. And, considering the wisdom and goodness of Almighty God, I cannot possibly believe but that all things necessary to be believed and practised by Christians in order to their eternal salvation are plainly contained in the Holy Scriptures. God surely hath not dealt so hardly with mankind as to make anything necessary to be believed or practised by us which he hath not made sufficiently plain to the capacity of the unlearned as well as of the learned. God forbid that it should be impossible for any man to be saved and get to heaven without a great deal of learning to direct and carry him thither, when the far greatest part of mankind have no learning at all. It was never well with the Christian world since it began to be a matter of so much subtlety and wit for a man to be a true Christian. —[i. 430.]

THE BIBLE TO BE REVERENCED

THE gravest book that ever was written may be made ridiculous by applying the sayings of it to a foolish purpose. For a jest may be obtruded upon anything. And therefore no man ought to have less reverence for the principles of religion or for the Holy Scriptures because idle and profane wits can break jests upon them. Nothing is so easy as to take particular phrases and expressions out of the best Book in the world, and to abuse them by forcing an odd and ridiculous sense upon them. But no wise man will think a good book foolish for this reason, but the man who abuses it; nor will he esteem that to which everything is liable to be a just exception against anything. At this rate we must despise all things, but surely the better and the shorter way is to contemn those who would bring anything that is worthy into contempt.—[i. 33.]

CHANCE NO EXPLANATION OF THE WORLD

WILL chance fit means to ends, and that in ten thousand instances, and not fail in any one? How often might a man, after he had jumbled a set of letters in a bag, fling them out upon the ground, before they would fall into an exact poem, yea or so much as make a good discourse in prose ?   And may not a little book be as easily made by chance as this great volume of the world ?   How long might a man be in sprinkling colours upon canvas with a careless hand before they would happen to make the exact picture of a man ?   And is a man easier made by chance than his picture ?   How long might twenty thousand blind men, which should be sent out from the remote parts of England, wander up and down before they would all meet upon Salisbury Plains and fall into rank and file in the exact order of an army ?   And yet this is much more easy to be imagined than how the innumerable blind parts of matter should rendez-vous themselves into a world.   A man that saw Henry the Seventh's chapel at Westminster [1] might with as good reason maintain (yea with much better, considering the vast difference betwixt that little structure and the huge fabric of the world) that it was never contrived or built by any man, but that the stones did by chance grow into those curious figures into which they seem to have been cut and graven, and that upon a time (as tales usually begin) the materials of that building, the stone, mortar,

---

[1] Described in Dean Stanley's *Memorials of Westminster Abbey*, ch. iii.

timber, iron, lead, and glass, happily met together and very fortunately ranged themselves into that delicate order in which we see them now so close compacted that it must be a very great chance that parts them again. What would the world think of a man that should advance such an opinion as this, and write a book for it ? If they would do him right, they ought to look on him as mad; but yet with a little more reason than any man can have to say that the world was made by chance, or that the first men grew up out of the earth as plants do now.—[i. 12.]

CHRISTIANITY

I WILL not deny but there are some persons as bad, nay perhaps worse, that have been bred up in the Christian religion than are commonly to be found in the darkness of paganism ; for the corruption of the best things is the worst, and those who have resisted so great a light as that of the gospel is, are likely to prove the most desperately wicked of all others. There is nothing that men make worse use of than of light and liberty, two of the best and most pleasant things in the world. Knowledge is many times abused to the worst purpose, and liberty into licentiousness and sedition; and yet no man for all that thinks ignorance desirable, or would wish a perpetual night and darkness to the world, and conclude, from the inconveniences of abused liberty, that the best state of things would be that the generality of mankind should be all slaves to a few and be perpetually chained to the oar or condemned to the mines. There are many times as bad consequences of good things as of bad, but yet there is a great difference between good and bad for all that.   As knowledge and liberty, so likewise the Christian religion is a great happiness to the world in general, though some are so unhappy as to be the worse for it— not because religion is bad, but because they are so.—[ii. 417.]

CHRISTIANITY AND CHRISTIANS

IT must be acknowledged to be a very untoward objection against the excellency and efficacy of the Christian religion, that the practice of so many Christians is so unequal to the perfection of their precepts.   For who is there in the changes and revolutions of human affairs, and when the wheel of providence turns them uppermost and lays their enemies at their feet, that will give them any quarter?   Nay, that does not greedily seize upon the first opportunities of revenge, and like an eagle hungry for his prey make a sudden stoop upon them with all his force and violence, and when he hath them in his pounces and at his mercy, is not ready to tear them to pieces ?

So that, after all our boasts of the excellency of our religion, where is the practice of it ? This, I confess, is a terrible objection indeed, and I must intreat of you, my brethren, to help me to the best answer to it, not by any nice distinctions and speculations about it, but by the careful and honest practice of this precept of our religion.

This was the old objection against philosophy, that many that were philosophers in their opinions were faulty in their lives. But yet this was never thought by wise men to be a good objection against philosophy. And unless we will lay more weight upon the objections against religion and press them harder than we think it reasonable to do in any other case, we must acknowledge likewise that this objection against religion is of no force. Men do not cast off the rules of physic because many physicians do not live up to their own rules and do not themselves follow those prescriptions which they think fit to give to others ; and there is a plain reason for it, because their swerving from their own rules doth not necessarily signify that their rules are not good, but only that their appetites are unruly and too hard and headstrong for their reason, nothing being more certain than this, that rules may be very reasonable and yet they that give them may not follow them.—[i. 310.]

CHRISTMAS AMUSEMENTS

WE cannot possibly choose a worse, a more improper season to sin in, than when we are celebrating the birth of the blessed Jesus who came to save us from our sins. This is as if a sick man, for joy that a famous physician is come to his house, should run into all manner of excess, and do all he can to inflame his disease and make his case desperate. Not but that our inward joy may lawfully be accompanied with all outward innocent expressions of it. But it is a matter of great scandal to our Saviour and his holy religion, that such irregular and extravagant things are at this time commonly done by many who call themselves Christians, and done under a pretence of doing honour to the memory of Christ's birth—as if, because the Son of God was at this time made man, it were fit for men to make themselves beasts.—[ii. 108.]

THE CHURCH, CATHOLIC OR ROMAN ?

THEY would have us to show them a society of Christians that in all ages has preserved itself free from all such errors and corruptions as we charge them withal, or else we deny the perpetual visibility of the catholic Church. No such matter. We say, the Church of Christ hath always been visible in every age since Christ's time, and that the several societies of Christians, professing the Christian doctrine and law of Christ, have made up the catholic Church, some parts whereof have in several ages fallen into great errors and corruptions—and no part of the catholic into more and greater than the church of Rome, so that it requires the utmost of our charity to think that they are a true, tho' a very unsound and corrupt, part of the catholic Church of Christ. We acknowledge likewise that we were once involved in the like degeneracy ; but by the mercy of God and pious care and prudence of those that were in authority, are happily rescued out of it. And tho' we were not out of the catholic Church before, yet since our reformation from the errors and corruptions of the church of Rome we are in it upon better terms and are a much sounder part of it ; and I hope, by the mercy and goodness of God, we shall for ever continue so.—[ii. 55, 56.]

THE CHURCH OF ROME

WHAT infallible security soever they have in the church of Rome, as to matters of faith, they are certainly the worst provided of wholesome and safe directions for the consciences and lives of men, of any church in the world. No religion that I know of in the world ever had such lewd and scandalous casuists. Witness the moral divinity of the Jesuits, which hath been so exposed to the world, not only by those of our religion but by their own writers also. Nor is this mischief only confined to that order; their casuists in general, and even the more ancient of them, who writ before the order of Jesuits appeared in the world, have given such a liberty and loose to great immorality in several kinds, as is infinitely to the reproach of the best and purest religion in the world. Insomuch that Sir Thomas More himself, who was a great zealot for that religion, could not forbear to make a loud complaint of it, and to pass this severe censure upon the generality of their casuists, 'that their great business seemed to be, not to keep men from sin, but to teach them how near to sin they might lawfully come, without sinning.' In the meantime the consciences of men are like to be well directed, when, instead of giving men plain rules for government of their lives and hearts, and clear resolutions of the material doubts which frequently occur in human life, they intangle them in niceties and endless scrupulosities, teaching them to split hairs in divinity and how with great art and cunning they may avoid the committing of any sin, and yet come as near to it as is possible ! This is a thing of the most dangerous consequence to the souls of men ; and if men be but once encouraged to pass to the utmost bounds of what is lawful, the next step will be into that which is unlawful.—[ii. 216, 217.]

CONFESSION

AS for our confessing our sins to men, both Scripture and reason do in some cases recommend and enjoin it.   As (i.) in order to the obtaining of the prayers of good men for us. *Confess your sins to one another*; he said before, *the prayer of faith shall save the sick, and the Lord shall raise him up* (James v. 16, 15). . . . (ii.) Confession of our sins to men is likewise reasonable in order to the ease and satisfaction of our minds, and our being directed in our duty for the future.   In this case, common reason and prudence, without any precept of Scripture, will direct men to have recourse to this remedy, viz. to discover and lay open our disease to some skilful spiritual physician, to some faithful friend or prudent guide, in order to spiritual advice, and direction, for the peace and satisfaction of our minds.   And then (iii.) in case our sins have been public and scandalous, both reason and the practice of the Christian Church do require that when men have publicly offended, they should give public satisfaction and open testimony of their repentance.

But as for private and auricular confession of our sins to a priest in all cases, and as of absolute necessity to our obtaining pardon and forgiveness from God, as the church of Rome teacheth, this is neither necessary by divine precept nor by any constitution and practice of the ancient Christian Church.—[iii. 17.]

There are many cases wherein men, under the guilt and trouble of their sins, can neither appease their own minds nor sufficiently direct themselves, without recourse to some pious and prudent guide ; in these cases men certainly do very well, and many times prevent a great deal of trouble and perplexity to themselves, by a timely discovery of their condition to some faithful minister, without which they shall never perhaps be able to clear themselves of the obscurity and entanglement of their own minds, but by smothering their troubles in their breasts shall proceed from one degree of melancholy to another, till at last they shall be plunged either into distraction or despair ; whereas the discovery of their condition in time would prove a present and effectual remedy. And to this purpose, a general confession is for the most part sufficient ; and where there is occasion for a more particular discovery, there is no need of raking into the particular and foul circumstances of men's sins, to give that advice which is necessary for the cure and ease of the penitent—a thing so far from being desirable, that it must needs be very grievous to every modest and good man.

And thus far confession is not only allowed but encouraged among Protestants.[1]—[iii. 11, 12.]

TWO DEFECTS OF OUR CHRISTIANITY

I WILL instance two great defects in the lives and practice of Christians, which are visible to every one, but are sad indications how little the power of religion prevails among men : I mean,

---

[1] This bears out Dr. Hensley Henson's judgment in his essay on Casuistry (in *English Religion in the Seventeenth Century*), that the practice of confession was common to Puritans and Anglicans : ' as to the practical wisdom of consulting a spiritual guide, the Puritan, who regarded the ordained minister as the Christian prophet, came not a whit behind the Anglican, who regarded him as a Christian priest. Both repudiated the Roman confessional with decision.'

the want of common honesty and integrity among
men, and the want of peace and love, the first of
which is the great virtue of civil conversation
[intercourse] and the other the great bond of civil
and ecclesiastical societies. These are two great
duties of religion frequently mentioned and strictly
charged upon the consciences of men in Scripture.
And yet how rare is the practice of them in the
lives of Christians !

(i.) The want of common honesty and integrity
among men. So indeed it used to be called,
' common ' honesty ; but it grows so rare now,
that it is like to lose that name ! Righteousness,
truth, and faithfulness are almost failed *from
among the children of men* ; all ranks of men have
corrupted themselves in this kind ; there is hardly
any trade or profession which hath not something
of knavery and falsehood woven into the very
mystery of it, and is become almost a necessary
part of it. Where is the generous honesty and
uprightness which did heretofore possess the spirits
of men, and which is an inseparable companion of
true courage ? But we are now passing apace
into foreign manners and vices, and any form of
religion will serve, when justice and integrity are
gone.

(ii.) The want of peace and love. How full of
factions and divisions are we ! And these managed

with all imaginable heat and animosity, one towards another, as if the badge of Christianity were changed and our Saviour had said, *Hereby shall all men know that ye are my disciples, if ye hate one another.* All the differences among Christians, of what denomination soever, are sadly to be lamented ; but I almost despair as to the differences between us and the church of Rome, because the reconciliation is impossible, unless they renounce their principles. They cannot come over to us, because they think they are infallible, and we cannot pass over to them, because we know they are deceived. So that there is a great gulf between us and them. We must not only renounce the Scriptures, but our reason and senses, to be of their mind. We cannot communicate with them in the sacrament, because they have taken away one half of it, which is as plainly instituted and commanded as the other part which is left. We cannot worship the Virgin Mary and the saints, much less their images, because it is written, *Thou shalt worship the Lord thy God, and him shalt thou serve. Thou shalt not make unto thyself any graven image, nor the likeness of anything that is in heaven above or in the earth beneath, or in the water under the earth ; thou shalt not bow down to them nor serve them ; for I the Lord thy God am a jealous God.* In short, several of their articles of faith are such as no credulity can swallow, and several parts of their worship are such as no piety can join with.[1] But this we bewail, that those who agree in the same essentials of faith and worship should be so forward to divide and separate from one another, merely upon forms of government and circumstances of worship.—[iii. 329, 330.]

THE DIFFICULTY OF GOODNESS

WHAT a conflict and struggling do the best men find between their inclinations and their duty! How hard to reconcile our practice and our knowledge, and to make our lives agree with the reason of our minds and the clear conviction of our consciences! How difficult for a man in this dangerous and imperfect state to be in any measure either so wise or good as he ought! How rare is it for a man to be good-natured, gentle, and easy to be entreated, without being betrayed into some weakness and sinful compliances, especially in the company of our betters! How next to impossible is it to be strict and severe in our lives, without being sour, to govern our lives with that

---

[1] Tillotson in his *Rule of Faith* describes the notorious Second Council of Nicæa, which in 787 ratified image-worship, as ' such a mess of fopperies, that if a general council of atheists had met together with a design to abuse religion by talking ridiculously concerning it, they could not have done it more effectually.'

perpetual caution and to maintain that evenness of temper and not to be sometimes peevish and passionate ! And when we are so, not to be apt to say with Jonah, *We do well to be angry*!—[ii. 261.]

DO IT NOW

CONSIDER that religion is a great and long work, and asks so much time that there is none left for the delaying of it. To begin with repentance, which is commonly our first entrance into religion, this alone is a great work, and is not only the business of a sudden thought and resolution, but of execution and action. . . . And do we think all this is to be done in an instant, and requires no time ? That we may delay and put off to the last, and yet do all this work well enough ? Do we think we can do all this in time of sickness and old age, when we are not fit to do anything, when the spirit of a man can hardly bear the infirmities of nature, much less a guilty conscience and a wounded spirit ? Do we think that when the day hath been idly spent and squandered away by us, we shall be fit to work when the night and darkness comes ? When our understanding is weak, and our memory frail, and our will crooked, and by a long custom of sinning obstinately bent

the wrong way, what can we then do in religion ?
What reasonable or acceptable service can we then
perform to God ?   When our candle is just sinking
into the socket, how shall our light *so shine before
men that others may see our good works* ?—[i. 120,
121.]

Where there is great hazard in the doing of a
thing, it is good to deliberate long before we undertake it.   But where the thing is not only safe but
beneficial, and not only beneficial but highly necessary, when our life and our happiness depends
upon it, and all the danger lies in the delay of it,
then we cannot be too sudden in our resolution
nor too speedy in the execution of it.   That which
is evidently safe needs no deliberation, and that
which is absolutely necessary will admit of none.
Therefore resolve upon it out of hand, *to-day, whilst
it is called to-day, lest any of you be hardened through
the deceitfulness of sin.*—[i. 261.]

EDUCATION

THERE are several ways of reforming men :
by the laws of the civil magistrate, and by
the public preaching of ministers.   But the most
likely and hopeful reformation of the world must

begin with children. Wholesome laws and good
sermons are but slow and late ways; the timely
and the most compendious way is a good education.
This may be an effectual prevention of evil, whereas
all other ways are but remedies which do always
suppose some neglect and omission of timely care.
—[i. 511.]

The first experiment that should be made upon
children should be to allure them to their duty,
and by reasonable inducements to gain them to the
love of goodness, by praise and reward, and sometimes by shame and disgrace. And if this will do,
there will be no occasion to proceed to severity,
especially not to great severities, which are very
unsuitable to human nature. A mixture of prudent
and seasonable reproof or correction, when there is
occasion for it, may do very well, but whips are not
the cords of a man; human nature may be driven
by them, but it must be led by sweeter and gentler
ways.

Great severities do often work an effect quite
contrary to that which was intended. And many
times those who were bred up in a very severe school
hate learning ever after, for the sake of the cruelty
that was used to force it upon them. So likewise
our endeavour to bring children to piety and goodness by unreasonable strictness and rigour does

often beget in them a lasting disgust and prejudice against religion. . . . Indeed, how can it be expected that children should love their duty, when they never hear of it but with a handful of rods shaked over them ?

I insist upon this the more, because I do not remember to have observed more notorious instances of miscarriage than in the children of very strict and severe parents ; of which I can give no other account but this, that nature, when it is thus overcharged, recoils the more terribly.—[i. 506, 507.]

Teach them some short and proper forms of prayer to God, to be said by them devoutly upon their knees in private, at least every morning and evening. A great many children neglect this, not from any ill disposition of the mind, but because nobody takes care to teach them how to do it.— [i. 502.]

I have known very careful and well-meaning parents that have with great severity restrained their children in the wearing of their hair. Nay, I can remember since the wearing of it below their ears was looked upon as a sin of the first magnitude, and when ministers generally, whatever their text was, did in every sermon either find or make an occasion with great severity to reprove the great sin of long hair ; and if they saw any one in the congregation guilty in that kind, they would point him out particularly and let fly at him with great zeal !

I have likewise known some parents that have strictly forbidden their children the use of some sorts of recreation and games, under the notion of heinous sins, upon a mistake that, because there was in them a mixture of fortune and skill, they were therefore unlawful—a reason which, I think, hath no weight and force in it, though I do not deny but human laws may for very prudent reasons either restrain or forbid the use of these games, because of the boundless expense both of money and time which is many times occasioned by them. . . .

These certainly are great mistakes, and many times have very pernicious effects, thus to confound things which are of so wide and vast a difference as good and evil, lawful and unlawful, indifferent and necessary. For when children come to be men and to have a freer and larger view of the world, and shall find, by the contrary practice of very wise and serious persons, that they have quite different apprehensions of these matters, and do not think that to be a sin which their parents have so strictly forbidden them under that notion, and many times punished them more severely for the doing of it than if they had told a lie, this may make them apt to question whether anything be a sin.—[i. 505.]

EMOTION

THE usual sign and outward expression of sorrow is tears; but these being not the substance of our duty, but an external testimony of it, which some tempers are more unapt to than others—we are much less to judge of the truth of our sorrow for sin by these than by our inward, sensible trouble and affliction of spirit. Some persons are of a more tender and melting disposition, and can command their tears upon a little occasion and upon very short warning; and such persons that can weep for everything else that troubles them have much more reason to suspect the truth of their sorrow for sin, if this outward expression of it be wanting. And we find in Scripture that the sorrow of true penitents does very frequently discover itself by this outward sign of it. . . .

But tho' this happen very frequently, yet it is not so constant and certain. For all men have not the same tenderness of spirit, nor are equally prone to tears; nay, tho' a man can weep upon natural accounts, as upon the loss of a child or near relation

or an intimate friend, or when he lies under a sharp
bodily pain, yet a man may truly repent, tho' he
cannot express his sorrow for sin the same way,
provided he give testimony of it by more real
effects.   And therefore the rule which is commonly
given by casuists in this case seems to be more
ensnaring than true and usual, namely ' that man
that can shed tears upon account of any evil less
than sin (as certainly all natural evils are) ought
to question the truth of his repentance for any
sin that he hath committed, if he cannot shed tears
for it.'   This, I think, is not true, because there is
scarce any man of so hard and unrelenting a spirit,
but the loss of a kind father or a dear child or other
near relation will force tears from him.   And yet
such a man, if it were to save his soul, may not be
able at some times to shed a tear for his sins.   And
the reason is obvious, because tears do proceed
from a sensitive trouble, and are commonly the
product of a natural affection ; and therefore 'tis
no wonder if they flow more readily and easily upon
a natural account, because they are the effect of a
cause suitable to their nature.   But sorrow for sin,
which hath more of the judgment and understanding in it, hath not its foundation in natural affection, but in reason, and therefore may not express
itself many times in tears, tho' it may produce
greater and more proper effects.

So that, upon the whole matter, I see no reason to call in question the truth and sincerity of that man's sorrow and repentance, who hates sin and forsakes it and returns to God and his duty, tho' he cannot shed tears and express the bitterness of his soul for his sin by the same significations that a mother doth in the loss of her only son. He that cannot weep like a child may resolve like a man ; and that undoubtedly will find acceptance with God.—[iii. 20, 21.]

THE EUCHARIST

'TIS true indeed, the danger of unworthy receiving is great ; but the proper inference and conclusion from hence is not that men should upon this consideration be deterred from the sacrament, but that they should be affrighted from their sins and from the wicked course of life which is an habitual indisposition and unworthiness. St. Paul indeed truly represents and very much aggravates the danger of the unworthy receiving this sacrament ; but he did not deter the Corinthians from it because they had sometimes come to it without due reverence, but exhorts them to mend what had been amiss and to come better prepared and disposed for the future. And therefore, after that terrible declaration in the text, *Whosoever shall eat this bread and drink this cup of the Lord unworthily, is guilty of the body and blood of the Lord*, he does not add, Therefore let Christians take heed of coming to the sacrament, but, Let them come prepared and with due reverence, not as to a common meal, but to a solemn participation of the body and blood of Christ : *but let a man examine himself, and so let him eat of that bread and drink of that cup.*—[i. 229.]

Our blessed Saviour plainly tells us that no sacrifice that we can offer will appease God towards us, so long as we ourselves are implacable to men. *If thou bring thy gift to the altar, and there rememberest that thy brother hath aught against thee, leave thy gift before the altar and go thy way ; first go and be reconciled to thy brother, and then come and offer thy gift.* To recommend this duty effectually to us, he gives it a preference to all the positive duties of religion : *first go and be reconciled to thy brother, and then come and offer thy gift.* Till this duty is discharged, God will accept of no service, no sacrifice at our hands. And therefore our liturgy doth with great reason declare it to be a necessary qualification for our worthy receiving the sacrament, that we be in 'love and charity with our neighbours,' because this is a moral duty and of eternal obligation, without which no positive part of religion, such as the sacraments are, can be acceptable to God, especially since in this blessed sacrament of Christ's Body and Blood we expect to have the forgiveness of our sins ratified and confirmed to us.   Which how can we hope for from God, if we ourselves be not ready to forgive one another ?—[i. 311.]

FACTION IN RELIGION

BY ' faction in religion ' I mean an unpeaceable and uncharitable zeal about things wherein religion either doth not consist at all, or but very little consists.   For besides that this temper is utterly inconsistent with several of the most eminent Christian virtues and graces, as humility, love, peace, meekness, and forbearance towards those that differ from us, it hath likewise two very great mischiefs commonly attending upon it, and both of them pernicious to religion and the souls of men.

First, that it takes such men off from minding the more necessary and essential parts of religion. They are so zealous about small things, the tithing of *mint and anise and cummin*, that they *neglect the weightier things of the Law,* faith and *mercy and judgment and the love of God,* and are so concern'd about little speculative opinions in religion, which they always call fundamental articles of faith, that the practice of religion is almost wholly neglected by them ; they are so taken up in spying and censuring error and heresy in others that they never think of curing those lusts and vices which do so visibly reign in themselves. Deluded people, that do not consider that the greatest heresy in the world is a wicked life, because it is so directly and fundamentally opposite to the whole design of the Christian faith and religion, and that do not consider that God will sooner forgive a man a hundred defects of his understanding than one fault of his will !

Secondly, another great mischief which attends this temper is, that men are very apt to interpret this zeal of theirs against others to be great piety in themselves and as much as is necessary to bring them to heaven, and think that they are very religious because they keep up a great stir about maintaining the outworks of religion, when it is ready to be starved within, and that there needs no more to denominate them good Christians but to be of such a church, which they always take to be the true one, and then zealously to hate and uncharitably to censure all the rest of mankind.

How many are there in the world that think they have made very sure of heaven, not by the old plain way of leaving their sins and reforming their lives, but by a more close and cunning way of carrying their vices along with them into another church and calling themselves ' good catholics ' and all others ' heretics ' ? . . .

Therefore, as thou valuest thy soul, take heed of engaging in any faction in religion.[1]—[i. 315, 316.]

THE FAITH OF ABRAHAM

THERE is one circumstance more especially which renders Abraham's obedience very remarkable : the deliberateness of the action. It had not been so much if, as soon as he had received this command from God, he had upon a sudden impulse and transport of zeal done this. But, that his obedience might be the more glorious and have all the circumstances of advantage given to it, God would have it done deliberately and upon full consideration ; and therefore he bade him go to the mountain three days' journey from the place where he was, and there to offer up his son.

It is in acts of virtue and obedience as in acts of sin and vice : the more deliberate the sin is, and

---

[1] So Richard Baxter closed his *Paraphrase of the New Testament* (1684) by writing, ' Readers, I earnestly advise you that you never take faction for religion.' He had been maligned by some ultra-Protestants for having refused to identify the Papacy and Antichrist. But he insisted, ' I dread the turning religion into a love-killing faction.'

the more calm and sedate temper the man is in when he commits it, the greater is the fault, whereas what is done by surprise, in the heat of temptation or transport of passion, hath some excuse from the suddenness and undeliberateness of it. So it is in acts of virtue and obedience, especially if they be attended with considerable difficulty ; the more deliberately they are done, the more virtuous they are, and the greater praise is due to them.

Now, that Abraham's obedience might want nothing to heighten it, God seems on purpose to have put so long a space betwixt the command and the performance of it ; he gives him time to cool upon it, to weigh the command and to look on every side of this difficult duty ; he gives scope for his reason to argue and debate the case, and opportunity for natural affection to play its part, and for flesh and blood to raise all its batteries against the resolution which he had taken up. And now we may easily imagine what conflict this good man had within himself during those three days that he was travelling to the mountain in Moriah, and how his heart was ready to be rent in pieces betwixt his duty to God and his affection to his child, so that every step of this unwelcome and wearisome journey he did, as it were, lay violent hands upon himself. He was to offer up his son but once, but he sacrificed himself and his own will every moment for three days together, and when he came thither and all things were now ready, the altar, the wood and the fire and the knife, it must needs be a stabbing question and wound him to the heart, which his innocent son so innocently asked him, *Where is the lamb for a burnt-offering ?* It must be a strong faith indeed and a mighty resolution that could make him to hold out for three days against the violent assaults of his own nature and the charming presence of his son, enough to melt his heart, as often as he cast his eyes upon him. And yet nothing of all this made him to stagger in his duty, but *being strong in faith he gave glory to God,* by one of the most miraculous acts of obedience that ever was exacted from any of the sons of men.—[ii. 12.]

I know not what some men may find in themselves, but I must freely acknowledge that I could never yet attain to the bold and hardy degree of faith as to believe anything for this reason, because it was impossible. For this would be to believe a thing to be, because I am sure it cannot be. So that I am very far from being of his [1] mind, that wanted not only more difficulties but even impossi-

---

[1] He means Sir Thomas Browne. In *Religio Medici* (i. 9) there is the famous outburst : ' Methinks there be not impossibilities enough in religion for an active faith, . . . I love to lose myself in a mystery, to pursue my reason to an *O Altitudo !* '

bilities in the Christian religion, to exercise his faith upon. 'Tis true indeed, Abraham, when he was offering up his son Isaac, is said *against hope* to have *believed in hope*. But he did not believe against a plain impossibility, for the apostle to the Hebrews expressly tells us that *he reasoned that God was able to raise him from the dead.*—[iii. 249.]

FAITH AND BELIEF

I DOUBT not but that there is so much evidence for the truth and divine authority of the gospel as is itself sufficient, without any peculiar operation of the Spirit of God, to silence all opposers and to convince them so far as that they cannot have any sufficient reason to disbelieve it; but withal I do not think that this faith doth become an abiding and effectual persuasion in any person, without the special operation of the Holy Ghost.—[iii. 434.]

Men do generally and without difficulty assent to mathematical truths, because it is nobody's interest to deny them; but men are slow to believe moral and divine truths, because by their lusts and interests they are prejudiced against them.—[i. 24.]

He who would persuade a man or prevail with him to do anything, must do it one of these three ways, either by entreaty or authority or argument ; either he must entreat him as a friend, or command him as subject to him and under his power, or convince him as a man.   Now, he that should go about to entreat men to believe anything or to charge them to do so, before he hath convinced them by sufficient arguments that it is reasonable to do so, would in my opinion take a preposterous course. He that entreats or charges a man to do anything, supposeth that he can do the thing if he will.   But a man cannot believe what he will ; the nature of a human understanding is such that it cannot assent without evidence nor believe anything to be true unless it see reason to do so, any more than a man can see a thing without light.   So that if the dearest friend that I have in the world should beg of me with the greatest importunity, or any man that hath the greatest authority over me should lay his severest commands upon me, to believe a thing for which I see no reason, I could not do it ; because nothing can command assent but evidence.   So that he who would persuade men to believe either the principles of natural religion or any divine revelation must convince them of the truth of them ; for it is unreasonable to desire a man to believe anything unless I give him good reason why he should. . . .

I know not how it comes to pass, but so it is, that every one that offers to give a reasonable account of his faith and to establish religion upon rational principles is presently branded for a Socinian.[1] Of which we have a sad instance in that incomparable person Mr. Chillingworth, the glory of this age and nation, who, for no other cause that I know of but his worthy and successful attempts to make Christianity reasonable religion and to discover [set forth] those firm and solid foundations upon which our faith is built, hath been requited with this black and odious character. But if this be Socinianism, for a man to enquire into the grounds and reasons of Christian religion and to endeavour to give a satisfactory account why he believes it, I know no way but that all considerate,[2] inquisitive[3] men, that are above fancy and enthusiasm, must be either Socinians or atheists.

I cannot imagine how men can do greater disservice to religion than by taking it off from the

---

[1] Some of Tillotson's clerical opponents called him bitterly a ' Socinian.' The truth was, he had offended them by being too broadminded. As Jortin sarcastically put it, Tillotson, in controverting the Socinians, broke ' an ancient and fundamental rule of theological controversy : *allow not an adversary to have either common sense or common honesty.*'

[2] thoughtful.   [3] enquiring.

rational and solid basis upon which it stands, and bearing the world in hand [1] that men ought to believe without reason ; for this is to turn faith into credulity and to level Christian religion with the vilest and most groundless enthusiasms that ever were in the world. Indeed, if we had only to deal with Henry Nicolas [2] and Jacob Behmen, who fight against us in the dark, not with reasons and arguments, but with insignificant [meaningless] words and obscure phrases, we might make a shift to bear up against them with this principle, and we might charge them to believe us, as they do us to believe them, without giving them any reason for it. But if we were to deal with Celsus or Julian or Porphyry or some of our modern atheists, we should soon find how vain it would be to go about to cajole them with phrases and to gain them over to Christianity by telling them that they must deny their reason and lay aside their understandings and believe, they know not why. If the great pillars of Christianity, the ancient fathers, had taken this course in their apologies for Christian

---

[1] To ' bear in hand ' is ' to delude.'

[2] An Amsterdam anabaptist, who started ' The Family of Love,' a mystical sect of ultra-spiritualists ; he seems to have claimed a divine mission. Behmen's writings had been translated into English by 1649 and 1651, and Behmenists were not unknown in the country. In the seventh chapter of his *Coming of the Friars*, Dr. Augustus Jessopp describes vividly these swarming visionaries.

religion, it had never triumphed over Judaism and paganism as it did. . . . They did very solicitously endeavour to satisfy the world by all rational ways, both of the truth and the reasonableness of Christian religion. And if that was a good way then, it is so now, and never more necessary than in this age, which I fear hath as many atheists and infidels that go under the name of Christians as ever were in any age since Christian religion was first planted in the world.—[iii. 442, 443.]

FAITH AND PROVIDENCE

OUR blessed Saviour, when he was ready to suffer, did not consider the malice of the Jews, which was the cause of his death, but looks to a higher hand : *the cup which my Father gives me to drink, shall I not drink it?* He that looks upon all things as coming from second causes, and does not eye the first cause, the good and wise Governor, will be apt to take offence at every cross and unwelcome accident. Men are apt to be angry when one flings water upon them as they pass in the streets, but no man is offended if he is wet by rain from heaven. When we look upon evils as coming only from men, we are apt to be impatient and know not how to bear them ; but we should look upon all things as under the government and disposal of the first cause, and the circumstances of every condition as allotted to us by the wise providence of God.   This consideration, that it is the hand of God and that he hath done it, would still all the murmurings of our spirits.   As when a seditious multitude is in an uproar, the presence of a grave and venerable person will hush the noise and quell the tumult ; so, if we would but represent God as present to all actions and governing and disposing all events, this would still and appease our spirits, when they are ready to riot and mutiny against any of his dispensations.—[ii. 693, 694.]

This is a proper expression of our confidence in God's wisdom and goodness, to refer things to him before the event, and to say with the Christians, *The will of the Lord be done*, because this shows that we are persuaded that God will do better for us than our own counsel and choice.   And to submit to his will after the event is likewise a great instance of our confidence in him.   And this may well be expected from us Christians who have much greater assurance of the particular providence of God than the heathens had.   And yet some of them were able to free themselves from all trouble and anxiety, from murmuring and discontent.   Upon this consideration, Epictetus (as Arrian tells us) would express himself thus : ' I had always rather have that which happens, because I esteem that better which God wills than that which I should will.' And again : ' Lift up thine eyes,' says he, ' with confidence to God, and say henceforth, " Lord, deal with me as thou pleasest : I am of the same opinion with thee, just of the same mind as that thou art : I refuse nothing that seems good to thee : lead me where thou wilt, clothe me with what garments thou pleasest, set me in a public place or keep me in a private condition, continue me in mine own country or banish me from it, bestow wealth upon me or leave me to conflict and struggle with poverty, which of these thou pleasest. If men shall censure this providence towards me and say thou dealest hardly with me, I will apologise for thee, I will undertake and maintain thy cause, that what thou dost is best for me." ' What could a Christian say more or better, by way of resignation of himself to the providence of God ? It almost transports me to read such passages from a heathen, especially if we consider in what condition Epictetus was ; he had a maimed and deformed body, was in the extremity of poverty, a slave, and cruelly and tyrannically used, so that we can hardly imagine a man in worse and more wretched circumstances ; and yet he justifies the providence of God in all this, and not only submits to his condition, but is contented with it and embraces it, and since God hath thought it fittest and best for him, he is of the same mind and thinks so too.   I confess it doth not move me to hear Seneca, who flowed with wealth and lived at ease, to talk magnificently and to slight poverty and pain as not worthy the name of evil and trouble.   But to see this poor man, in the lowest condition and worst circumstances of humanity, bear up so bravely and with such cheerfulness and serenity of mind to entertain his hard fortune, and this not of stupidity but from a wise sense of the providence of God and a firm persuasion of the wisdom and goodness of all his dealings —this, who can choose but be affected with it as an admirable temper for a Christian, much more for a heathen? To which we may apply the saying of our Lord concerning the heathen centurion, *Verily, I say unto you, I have not found so great faith, no, not in Israel*; so wise, so equal, so firm a temper of mind is seldom to be found, no, not amongst Christians.— [ii. 562, 563.]

FAITH'S WEAK POINT

HOW few there are that believe and hope and fear concerning the things of another world as *the children of this world* do concerning the things of this world!   If any man ask me how I know this,

I appeal to experience. It is plain and visible in the lives and actions and endeavours of men. Good men are seldom so effectually and throughly persuaded of the principles of religion and the truth of the sayings contained in the holy Scriptures as the men of the world are of their own sayings and proverbs. Men do not believe that honesty is the best policy, or (as Solomon expresseth it) that *he that walketh uprightly walketh surely*, as the men of the world believe their own maxims that ' a man may be too honest to live,' that ' plain-dealing is a jewel, but he that wears it shall die a beggar.' Few men's hopes of heaven are so powerful and vigorous, and have so sensible an effect upon their lives, as the worldly man's hopes of gain and advantage. Men are not so afraid to swear as they are to speak treason; they are not so firmly persuaded of the danger of sin to their souls and bodies in another world as of the danger to which some crimes against the laws of men do expose their temporal lives and safety.—[ii. 487.]

FEAR AS A RELIGIOUS MOTIVE

THERE are two bridles or restraints which God hath put upon human nature, shame and fear. Shame is the weaker, and hath place only in those in whom there are some remainders of virtue. Fear is the stronger, and works upon all who love themselves and desire their own preservation. Therefore in this degenerate state of mankind fear is that passion which hath the greatest power over us, and by which God and his laws take the surest hold of us; our desire and love and hope are not so apt to be wrought upon by the representations of virtue and the promises of reward and happiness as our fear is from the apprehensions of divine displeasure. For though we have lost in a great measure the gust and relish of true happiness, yet we still retain a quick sense of pain and misery. Therefore religion usually makes its first entrance into us by this passion.— [i. 2.]

It is plain from Scripture that God propounds to men several motives and arguments to obedience, some proper to work upon their fear, as the threatenings of punishment, some upon their hope, as the promises of blessing and reward, others upon their love, as the mercies and forgiveness of God. From whence it is evident he intended they should all work upon us. And accordingly the Scripture gives us instances in each kind. Noah *moved with fear* obeyed God *in preparing an ark.* Moses had *respect unto the recompence of the reward.* Mary

Magdalene *loved much*. And as it is hard to say, so it is not necessary to determine, just how much influence and no more each of these hath upon us ; it is very well if men be reclaimed from their sins and made good by the joint force of all the considerations which God offers to us. To be sure, love is the noblest and most generous principle of obedience, but fear commonly takes the first and fastest hold of us, and, in times of violent temptation, is perhaps the best argument to keep even the best of men within the bounds of their duty.—[i. 132.]

It is not against the genius of true religion to urge men with arguments of fear. No man can imagine there would have been so many fearful threatenings in Scripture, and especially in the gospel, if it had not been intended they should have some influence upon us. Some look upon all arguments of fear as legal, as contrary to the genuine spirit and temper of the gospel, and look upon preachers who urge men with considerations taken from the justice of God and the terrors of the Lord, as of an unevangelical spirit. But will such men allow our Saviour and his apostles to have been evangelical preachers ? If so, it is not contrary to the gospel to use arguments of terror. They thought them very proper to deter men from sin and to bring them to repentance. *Knowing therefore the terrors of the Lord, we persuade men.* Some are so tender that they cannot bear any other arguments but such as are taken from the free grace of God and the free love of Christ ; if we mention to them the wrath of God and the torments of hell, we grate upon them. But if we consider the primitive preaching of Christ and his apostles, we must allow the necessity and usefulness of those arguments.

And indeed, if we consider the nature and reason of things, nothing is more apt to work upon sinners than arguments of fear. Fear is deeply rooted in our nature, and immediately flows from that principle of self-preservation which is planted in every man. 'Tis the most wakeful passion in the soul of man, and so soon as anything that is dreadful and terrible is presented to us, it alarms us to flee from it. And this passion doth naturally spring up in our minds from the apprehension of a Deity, because the notion of a God doth include in it power and justice, both which are terrible to guilty creatures. So that fear is intimate to our being, and God hath hid in every man's conscience a secret awe and dread of his presence, of his infinite power and eternal justice. Now, fear being one of the first things that is imprinted upon us from the apprehension of a Deity, it is that passion which

above all others gives the greatest advantage to
religion. . . . Fear is a good sure principle, and
one of the best guards and securities against sin ;
other passions are fickle and inconstant, but we
cannot shake off our fears, nor quit ourselves of
them, so long as we believe the reality of the
object. There will be fear and terror in a guilty
conscience, so long as it believes in a holy, just,
and omnipotent God, and that *it is a fearful
thing to fall into the hands of the living God.*—[iii.
605, 606.]

It seems a very hard case that when we have to
deal with men, sensible enough of their interest
in other cases and diligent enough to mind it, we
cannot persuade them to accept of happiness without setting before them the terrors of the eternal
darkness and those amazing and endless miseries
which will certainly be the portion of those who
refuse so great an happiness : this, I say, seems
hard, that men must be carried to the gate of hell
before they can be brought to set their faces towards
heaven and to think in good earnest of getting
thither.[1]—[iii. 44.]

[1] Sir Thomas Browne thought otherwise. ' I can hardly think there
was ever any scared into heaven ; they go the fairest way to heaven that
would serve God without a hell ' (*Religio Medici*, lii.).

FORGIVENESS

I HAVE sometimes wondered how it should come to pass that so many persons should be so apt to despair of the mercy and forgiveness of God to them, especially considering what clear and express declarations God hath made of his readiness to forgive our greatest sins and provocations upon our sincere repentance. But the wonder will be very much abated, when we shall consider with how much difficulty men are brought to remit great injuries, and how hardly we are persuaded to refrain from flying upon those who have given us any considerable provocation. . . . The best way to keep ourselves from despairing of God's mercy and forgiveness to us, is to be easy to grant forgiveness to others. And without that, as God hath reason to deny forgiveness to us, so we ourselves have all the reason in the world utterly to despair of it. . . .

Enable us, O Lord, to practise this excellent and difficult duty of our religion. And then *forgive us our trespasses, as we forgive them that trespass against us,* for thy mercy's sake in Jesus Christ, to whom, with thee, O Father, and the Holy Ghost, be all honour and glory, adoration and obedience, both now and ever. Amen.—[i. 312.]

THE ATTRIBUTES OF GOD

WHEN Moses desires to *see God's glory*, he tells him that he will *cause all his goodness to pass before him*. Without goodness, the power and wisdom of God would be terrible, and raise great dread and superstition in the minds of men. Without goodness, power would be tyranny and oppression, and wisdom would degenerate into craft and mischievous contrivance. So that a Being endowed with all power and wisdom, and yet wanting goodness, would be a dreadful and omnipotent mischief. We are apt to dread power and to admire knowledge and to suspect great wisdom and prudence ; but we can heartily love and reverence nothing but true goodness. 'Tis not the infinite power and knowledge of God, considered abstractly and in themselves, but these in conjunction with his great goodness, that make him at once the most awful and amiable Being in the world. Which is the reason why our Saviour speaks of the mercy and goodness and patience of God as the top and sum of the divine perfections ; *be ye therefore perfect, as your Father which is in heaven is perfect.* How is that ? In being *good to the unthankful and evil*, as God is who *makes his sun to rise and his rain to fall not only on just but unjust.* And therefore St. Luke renders it, *Be ye therefore merciful, as your Father in heaven is merciful.* To be good and merciful, as God is, is to be perfect as he is, because it is to imitate him in that which is his chief perfection.— [iii. 372.]

Do not consider God as mere power and sovereignty, as mere mercy and goodness, as mere justice and severity, but as all these together, and in such a measure and degree as may make them consistent with one another. The greatest mistakes in religion are certainly sprung from this root, from separating the perfections of God and considering them singly and framing such wide and large notions of one as to exclude another ; whereas the perfections of God agree together, and that is not a divine perfection which contradicts any other perfection. Among men indeed an eminent degree of any one excellency does usually shut out some other ; and therefore it is observed that power and moderation, love and discretion, do not often meet together, that a great memory and a small judgment, a good wit and an ill nature, are many times found in conjunction. But in infinite perfection all perfections do eminently meet and consist together, and it is not necessary that one excellency should be raised upon the ruins of another.

And if this had been well considered, men would not, by being too intent upon God's sovereignty, with neglect of his other perfections, have spoken those hard things about predestination; for the sovereignty of God doth by no means set him above the eternal law of goodness and truth and righteousness. And if this were considered, men would not, by poring upon the justice and severity of God, be so swallowed up in despair; for God is not so severe but he is merciful to the penitent, and hath left a retreat for the returning sinner. If this were well considered, it would check the presumption of those who encourage themselves in sin by fancying to themselves a God all of mercy and goodness, and *because sentence against an evil work is not speedily executed, therefore their heart is set in them to do evil*; for it is not goodness and mercy finally to bear with and forgive obstinate offenders, but want of prudence and good government.—[ii. 494, 495.]

God would save us any way, by his mercy or by his judgment, by sickness or by health, by plenty or by want, by what we desire or by what we dread; so desirous is he of our repentance and happiness that he leaves no method unattempted that may probably do us good, he strikes upon every passion in the heart of man, he works upon our love by his goodness, upon our hopes by his promises, and upon our fears first by his threatenings and, if they be not effectual, then by his judgments; he tries every affection and takes hold of it, if by any means he may draw us to himself.—[ii. 657.]

GOD'S GREAT MERCY

IF we look into ourselves and consider our own temper and disposition, how void of pity we are, how cruel and hard-hearted and insolent and revengeful, if we look abroad in the world and see how full the earth is of *the habitations of cruelty*, we shall admire the mercy of God more and think ourselves the more beholden to it.   How many things must concur to make our hearts tender and melt our spirits, to make us pitiful and compassionate! We seldom pity any unless they be actually in misery; nor all such neither, unless the misery they lie under be very great; nor then neither, unless the person that suffers be nearly related, and we be some ways concerned in his sufferings; yea, many times not then neither, upon a generous account, but as we are some ways obliged by interest and self-love and a dear regard for ourselves, when we have suffered the like ourselves and we have learned to pity others by our own sufferings, or when in danger and probability to be in the like condition ourselves. So many motives and obligations are necessary to awaken and stir up this affection in us. But God is merciful and pitiful to us out of the mere goodness of his nature ; for few of these motives and considerations can have any place in him. This affection of pity and tenderness is stirred up in God by the mere presence of the object, without any other inducement. The mercy of God many times doth not stay till we be actually miserable, but looks forward a great way and pities us. God doth not only pity us in great calamities, but considers those lesser evils that are upon us. God is merciful to us, when we have deserved all the evils that are upon us and far greater, when we *are less than the least of all his mercies*, when we deserved all the misery that is upon us, and have with violent hands pulled it upon our own heads, and have been the authors and procurers of it to ourselves.—[ii. 628.]

GRACE AT MEALS

I MUST by no means omit, because it is in many families already gone and in others going out of fashion—I mean, a solemn acknowledgment of the providence of God by begging his blessing at our meals, upon his good creatures provided for our use, and by returning thanks to him for the benefit and refreshment of them, this being a piece of natural religion owned and practised in all ages and in most places of the world, but never so shamefully and scandalously neglected and, I fear, by many slighted and despised, as it is amongst us at this day. And most neglected where there is greatest reason for the doing of it, I mean, at the most plentiful tables and amongst those of highest quality; as if great persons were ashamed or thought scorn to own from whence these blessings come, like the nation of the Jews, of whom God complains in the prophet, *she knew not that I gave her corn and wine and oil, and multiplied her silver and gold*; *she knew not*, that is, she would not acknowledge from whose bounty all these blessings came.—[i. 480.]

HEAVEN

WE read, *and his servants shall serve him and they shall see his face.* In which last words our employment and our happiness are expressed; but what in particular our employment shall be, and wherein it shall consist, is impossible now to describe. It is sufficient to know in the general that our employment shall be our unspeakable pleasure, and every way suitable to the glory and happiness of that state, and as much above the noblest and most delightful employments of this world as the perfection of our bodies and the power of our souls shall then be above what they now are in this world. For there is no doubt but that he who made us and endued our souls with a desire of immortality and so large a capacity of happiness, does understand very well by what ways and means to make us happy, and hath in readiness proper exercises and employments for that state, and every way more fitted to make us happy than any condition or employment in this world is suitable to a temporal happiness. I will say no more upon this argument, lest I should say less, and because whoever ventures to wade far into it will soon find himself out of his depth and in danger to be swallowed up and lost in that great abyss, which is not to be fathomed by the shallow faculties of mortal men.—[iii. 58.]

HEAVEN NOT A HOSPITAL

LET us not deceive ourselves. Heaven is not a hospital made to receive all sick and aged persons that can but put up a faint request to be admitted there. No, no, they are never like to see the kingdom of God, who, instead of seeking it in the first place, make it their last refuge and retreat, and when they find the sentence of death upon them, only to avoid present execution, do bethink themselves of getting to heaven, and, since there is no other remedy, are contented to petition the great King and Judge of the world that they may be transported thither.—[iii. 30.]

Do not delude yourselves with vain hopes that this work may be done at any time and in an instant, and that if you can but fashion your last breath into *Lord, have mercy upon me,* this will prevail with God and make atonement for the long course of a wicked and sinful life. What strange thoughts have men of God and heaven, what extravagant conceits of the little evil of sin and the easiness of repentance, that can impose upon themselves at this rate! Bethink yourselves better in time, *consider and show yourselves men.* What will you do in the day of your distress, who have neglected God in your most flourishing and prosperous condition? What will you say to him in a dying hour, who scarce ever had one serious thought of him all your life? Can you have the face at that time to bespeak him in this manner? —' Lord, now the world and my lusts have left me,

and I feel myself ready to sink into eternal perdi-
tion, I lay hold upon thy mercy to deliver my soul
from going down into the pit.   I have heard strange
things of thy goodness, and that thou art merciful,
even to a miracle. This is that which I always
trusted to, that after a long life of sin and vanity
thou wouldest at last be pacified with a few penitent words and sighs at the hour of death. Let
me not, I pray thee, be disappointed of this hope
and put to confusion.' Is this an address fit to be
made to a wise man, much less to the all-wise and
just Judge of the world ? And yet this seems
to be the plain interpretation of the late and forced
application of a great and habitual sinner to
almighty God in his last extremity, and when he
is just giving up the ghost and going to appear
before his dread tribunal. I say again, let no man
deceive you with vain words or vain hopes or false
notions of a slight and sudden repentance. As if
heaven were a hospital founded on purpose to
receive all sick and maimed persons that, when
they can live no longer to the lusts of the flesh and
the sinful pleasures of this world, can but put up
a cold and formal petition to be admitted there.
No, no, as sure as God is true, they shall never see
the kingdom of God who, instead of seeking it in
the first place, make it their last refuge and retreat !
The ever-blessed God is himself abundantly suffi-

cient for his own happiness, and does not need our company to make any addition to it. Nor yet is heaven so desolate a place or so utterly void of inhabitants that, like some newly discovered plantation,[1] it should be glad to receive the most vile and profligate persons, the scum and refuse of mankind. There are an innumerable company of glorious angels, much nobler creatures than the best of men, to people those blessed regions, *thousands of thousands* continually *standing before God* and *ten thousand times ten thousand ministering unto him.*

To conclude. If we would have God to accept us in a dying hour, and our blessed Saviour to remember us, now he is in his kingdom, let us think of him betimes and *acquaint ourselves with him that we may be at peace*—now, before *the evil days come and the years draw nigh when we shall say, we have no pleasure in them. O that men were wise, that they understood this, that they would consider their latter end.* Which God of his infinite goodness grant that we may all seriously lay to heart in this our day, and may learn betimes *so to number our days that we may apply our hearts*

---

[1] A colony or settlement. ' It is a shameful and unblessed thing to take the scum of people and wicked condemned men, to be the people with whom you plant,' says Bacon in his essay on *Plantations*, referring like Tillotson to the class of people often settled by the English in their new territories across the Atlantic.

to wisdom, for his mercies' sake in Jesus Christ, to whom with the Father and the Holy Ghost be all honour and glory, now and for ever. Amen.—[i. 522, 523.]

HYPOCRISY

A MERE form of religion does upon some accounts bring a man under a heavier sentence than if he were openly profane and irreligious. He that makes a show of religion flatters God, but all the while he acts and designs against him ; whereas the profane man deals plainly, and tho' he be a monstrous and unnatural rebel, yet he is a fair and open enemy. And the kisses of a false friend are more hateful than the wounds of an open enemy. . . . I will not deny but that a profane man is a worse example to the world, and may do more mischief upon that account ; but the hypocrite is more mischievous to himself, and of the two more odious to God, and sometimes does more prejudice to religion by undermining it than the other does by all his open assaults and batteries. God cannot endure to be affronted, but he hates to be mocked.—[iii. 327.]

THE JUDGMENTS OF GOD

M EN are very apt to make this bad use of the signal judgments of God upon others. This our Saviour plainly intimates in the text, *Suppose ye that these* Galileans *were sinners above all the Galileans, because they suffered such things ? Or these eighteen upon whom the tower of Siloam fell, think ye that they were sinners above all that dwelt in Jerusalem ?* By which manner of speaking our Saviour signifies that men are very apt thus to suppose that those upon whom the extraordinary judgments of God fall are no ordinary sinners but are guilty of somewhat above the common rate of men. . . . And we find in common experience how prone men are to make uncharitable constructions of the judgments of God upon others and grievously to censure those whom God hath smitten, partly because it looks like a vindication of themselves from the guilt of the like crimes, since they are not involved in the like sufferings, partly to gratify their pride and curiosity, in seeming to understand the reason and end of God's judgments, as if they had been of his council and saw further into the reasons of his providence than other men. . . . Or lastly, men think it a piece of piety and affectionate zeal for God and a taking of his part, to censure those heavily whom God afflicts severely—like some foolish parasites who, if they see a great man be angry with any one and strike him, they think themselves bound to fall upon him and, out of an officious flattery, will beat him too. But from whatever cause it proceeds, it is certainly a very bad thing, and our Saviour here in the text does with great vehemence deny that any such conclusion can certainly be collected from the judgments of God upon others: *I tell you, Nay.* And to express this more vehemently, he repeats it again, *I tell you, Nay.*

Let us more particularly consider some of the rash conclusions which men are apt to draw from the judgments of God upon others, whether upon public societies and communities of men or upon particular persons.

It is rash, where there is no divine revelation in the case, to be peremptory as to the particular sin or kind of it, so as to say that for such a sin God sent such a judgment upon a particular person or upon a company of men, unless the judgment be a natural effect and consequence of such a sin. . . . Thus the Papists, on the one hand, attribute all the judgments of God upon this nation, the confusion and distractions of so many years, and those late judgments wherewith God hath visited us in so dreadful a manner, to our schism and heresy as the proper cause of them (for so they call our reformation of ourselves from their errors and corruptions). But to what cause then will they ascribe the great felicity of Queen Elizabeth's long reign, and the peace of King James his reign? And then, on the other hand, some of the dissenters from our Church are wont to ascribe these calamities to a quite different cause, that our reformation hath not gone far enough from the church of Rome. It is hard to say which of these conclusions is most rash and unreasonable. I wish other reasons of these calamities were not too visible and notorious —the horrible impiety and wickedness which abounds and reigns amongst us.

It is rash likewise for any man without revelation to conclude peremptorily that God must needs in his judgments only have regard to some late and fresh sins, which were newly committed, and that all his arrows are only levelled against those impieties of men which are now upon the stage and in present view. This is rash and groundless; and men herein take a measure of God by themselves, and, because they are mightily affected with the present and sensible of a fresh provocation, and want to revenge themselves while the heat is upon them, therefore they think God must do so too. But there is nothing occasions more mistakes in the world about God and his providence than to bring him to our standards and to measure his thoughts by our thoughts and the ways and methods of his providence by our ways. Justice in God is a wise and calm and steady principle, which as to the time and circumstances of its exercise is regulated by his wisdom. Past and present are very material differences to us, but they signify little to God, whose vast and comprehensive understanding takes in all differences of time and looks upon them in one view, so that, when the judgments of God follow the sins of men at a great distance, *God is not slack, as men count slackness ; for a thousand years in his sight are but as one day, and one day as a thousand years*, as the apostle reasons about this very case.—[iii. 624, 625.]

The judgments of God, which are many times abroad in the earth, are nothing else but the wise methods which the great Physician of the world uses for the cure of mankind. . . . It may be there are some sinners which are more tractable and easy to be reduced to goodness, that are not so headstrong and obstinate in their way but that they may be reclaimed by milder and softer means. But there are likewise a great many senseless and outrageous sinners who are madly and furiously bent upon their own ruin. Now to treat them fairly, with the allurements of kindness and the gentle arts of persuasion, would be to no purpose ; the only way that is left of dealing with them is rigour and severity.   When sinners are thus beside themselves, something that looks like cruelty is perhaps the greatest mercy that can be shown to them ; nothing so proper for such persons as a dark room and a spare diet and severe usage.—[i. 83.]

God many times suffers the most grievous sins of particular persons to go unpunished in this world, because he knows that his justice will have another and better opportunity to meet and reckon with them.   But the general and crying sins of a nation cannot hope to escape public judgments, unless they be prevented by a general repentance.   God may defer his judgments for a time, and give a people a longer space of repentance ; he may stay till the iniquities of a nation be full, but sooner or later they have reason to expect his vengeance. And usually the longer punishment is delayed, it is the heavier when it comes.

Now all this is very reasonable, because this world is the only season for national punishments.   And indeed they are in a great degree necessary for the present vindication of the honour and majesty of the divine laws, and to give some check to the overflowing of wickedness.   Public judgments are the banks and shores upon which God breaks the insolency of sinners and stays their proud waves. And though among men the multitude of offenders be many times a cause of impunity, because of the weakness of human governments which are glad to spare where they are not strong enough to punish, yet in the government of God things are quite otherwise. No combination of sinners is too hard for him, and the greater and more numerous the offenders are, the more his justice is concerned to vindicate the affront. However God may pass by single sinners in this world, yet when a nation combines against him, *when hand joins in hand, the wicked shall not go unpunished.*—[i. 36.]

LOVE YOUR ENEMIES

IF we could be impartial and lay aside prejudice, we might perhaps discern several very lovely qualities in him who hates us—and virtue is to be owned and praised and loved even in an enemy. And perhaps his enmity towards us is not so great and inexcusable a fault as we apprehend ; he is not perhaps our enemy to that degree, nor so altogether without cause as we imagine ; possibly we have provoked him, or by his own mistake or through the malicious representation of others he may be induced to think so. And are we not ourselves liable to the like misapprehensions concerning others, of which we are many times afterwards convinced and ashamed ? And so may he ; and then his enmity will cease, if we will but have a little patience with him, as we always wish in the like case that others would have with us.

At the worst, tho' never so sore and causeless an enemy, tho' never so bad a man, yet he is a man, and as such hath something in him which the blindest passion cannot deny to be good and amiable. He hath the same nature with ourselves, which we cannot hate or despise without hatred and con- tempt of ourselves. Let a man's faults be what they will, they do not destroy his nature and make him cease to be a man. . . .

Consider further that an enemy, even whilst he is exercising his enmity towards us, may do us many acts of real advantage, which, though they do not proceed from kindness, yet in truth are benefits. The malicious censures of our enemies, if we make a right use of them, may prove of greater advantage to us than the civilities of our best friends.[1]—[i. 304, 305.]

---

[1] John Evelyn heard this sermon preached on March 8, 1689: ' an excellent discourse on Matthew v. 44, exhorting to charity and forgiveness of enemies ; I suppose purposely, the new Parliament being furious about impeaching those who were obnoxious, and, as their custom hath ever been, going on violently, without reserve or moderation, whilst wise men were of opinion, the most notorious offenders being named and excepted, an Act of Amnesty would be more seasonable to pacify the minds of men in so general a discontent of the nation.'

WHAT IS MAN ?

CONSIDER man by himself, and from under the conduct and protection of a superior and more powerful Being, and he is in a most disconsolate and forlorn condition, secure of nothing he enjoys, and liable to be disappointed of everything that he hopes for ; he is apt to grieve for what he cannot help, and perhaps the justest cause of his grief is that he cannot help it ; for if he could, instead of grieving for it he would help it. He cannot refrain from desiring a great many things which he would fain have, but is never likely to obtain, because they are out of his power ; and it troubles him both that they are so, and that he cannot help his being troubled at it. Thus man walketh in a vain show, and *disquieteth himself in vain*, courting happiness in a thousand shapes, and the faster he follows it, the swifter it flies from him. Almost everything promiseth happiness to us at a distance, such a step of honour, such a pitch of estate, such a fortune or match for a child ; but when we come nearer to it, either we fall short of it, or it falls short of our expectation ; and it is hard to say which of these is the greatest disappointment. . . .

And when we are grown up, we are liable to a

great many mischiefs and dangers every moment
of our lives, and, without the providence of God,
continually insecure not only of the good things
of this life but even of life itself; so that when
we come to be men, we cannot but wonder [1] how
ever we arrived at that state, and how we have
continued in it so long, considering the infinite
difficulties and dangers which have continually
attended us : that in running the gantlope [gaunt-
let] of a long life, when so many hands have been
lifted against us, and so many strokes levelled at
us, we have escaped so free and with so few marks
and scars upon us : that when we are besieged
with so many dangers, and so many arrows of
death are perpetually flying about us, to which
we do so many ways lie open, we should yet hold
out twenty, forty, sixty years, and some of us
perhaps longer, and do still stand at the mark
untouched, at least not dangerously wounded by
any of them : and, considering likewise this fearful
and wonderful frame of a human body, this infinitely
complicated engine, in which, to the due performance of the several functions and offices of life, so
many strings and springs, so many receptacles and

---

[1] Jowett, in his *Biographical Sermons* (pp. 80 f.), makes a similar remark,
speaking about an old man's view of his past life : ' He wonders how he
ever escaped from the temptations of youth, and is sometimes inclined to
think that the Providence which watches over children and drunken people
must have had a special care of him.'

channels, are necessary, and all in their right frame and order, and in which, besides the infinitely imperceptible and secret ways of mortality, there are so many sluices and flood-gates to let death in and life out, that it is next to a miracle, tho' we take but little notice of it, that every one of us did not die every day since we were born : I say, considering the wise and curious hazard of our bodies and the innumerable contingencies and hazards of human life, which is set in so slippery a place, that we still continue in the land of the living, we cannot ascribe to anything but the watchful providence of Almighty God, who *holds our soul in life and suffers not our foot to be moved.*—[i. 376, 377.]

RELIGIOUS MELANCHOLY

THEY who are under the power of it are seldom fit to take that counsel which alone is fit to be given them ; and that is, not to believe themselves concerning themselves, but to trust the judgment of others rather than their own apprehensions. In other cases every man knows himself best, but a melancholy man is most in the dark as to himself. This cause of trouble and doubting is very much to be pitied, but hard to be removed, unless by physic or by time or by chance.

One may happen to say something that may hit the humour of a melancholy man and satisfy him for the present ; but reason must needs signify very little to those persons the nature of whose distemper it is to turn everything that can be said for their comfort into objections against themselves.—[i. 133.]

There are many [1] who, being of a dark and melancholy temper, are apt to represent things worse to themselves than there is reason for, and do many times fancy themselves guilty of great crimes in the doing or neglecting of those things which in their nature are indifferent, and are apt to aggravate and blow up every little infirmity into an unpardonable sin. Most men are apt to extenuate their sins, and not to be sensible enough of the evil and heinousness of them ; but it is the peculiar infelicity of melancholy persons to look upon their faults as blacker and greater than in truth they are, and whatsoever they hear and read in Scripture that is spoken against the grossest and most enormous offenders, they apply to themselves.—[ii. 433.] [2]

[1] In his autobiography for 1671 Richard Baxter notes : ' I was troubled this year with multitudes of melancholy persons from several parts of the land, some of high quality, some of low, some very exquisitely learned, some unlearned.'

[2] Macaulay has pointed out, from the *Pilgrim's Progress*, ' how strong a sympathy Bunyan felt, after his mind had become clear and cheerful, for persons afflicted with religious melancholy.'

RELIGIOUS METAPHORS

I DO not love to hunt down a metaphor; for I know very well that the Scripture (like other authors) useth a metaphor only to one purpose at one time; and tho' many more similitudes may by fancy be found out, it is certain but one is intended. Which I take notice of, on purpose to reprove the vanity and injudiciousness of chasing metaphors farther than ever they were intended. For a metaphor is commonly used to represent to our mind the first and most obvious likeness of things.—[iii. 552.]

After a man hath delivered the simple notion of a thing in proper words, he may afterwards illustrate it by metaphors, but then these are not to be insisted upon and strained to the utmost extent of the metaphor, beyond what the true notion of the thing will bear. For if consequences once come to be drawn from metaphors, and doctrines founded and theories built upon them, instead of illustrating the thing, they blind and obscure it, and serve to no other purpose but to seduce and mislead the understandings of men and to multiply controversies without end.—[iii. 463.]

I will add this concerning Scripture-metaphors in general, that where the Scripture useth metaphors which were very familiar in those languages in which the Scripture was writ, and well understood by those who spoke that language, but are very obscure and uncouth to us and not at all used in our language, as most of the Scripture-metaphors are, the proper work of a minister is not to insist in such cases upon Scripture-metaphors, to darken his discourses by them, but to explain them and make them intelligible, to translate them into English, and instead of them to use such phrases as people are more familiarly acquainted with and are used in our own language. For a man may be a barbarian, that speaks to people in unknown phrases and metaphors, as well as *he that speaks in an unknown tongue*; and the very same reason that obligeth us to put the Scripture into a known language doth oblige us men to explain the doctrines contained in it by such phrases and metaphors as are known and used in that language.— [iii. 464.]

MIRACLES

MIRACLES are the highest attestation that can be given to the truth and divinity of any doctrine; and supposing a doctrine not to be plainly unworthy of God and contrary to those natural notions which men have of God and religion, we can have no greater evidence of the truth of it than miracles; they are such an argument as in its own nature is apt to persuade and induce belief.

All truths do not need miracles. Some are of easy belief, and are so clear by their own light that they need neither miracle nor demonstration to prove them. Such are those self-evident principles which mankind do generally agree in ; others, which are not so evident by their own light, we are content to receive upon clear demonstration of them, or very probable arguments for them, without a miracle. And there are some truths which, however they may be sufficiently obscure and uncertain to most men, yet are they so inconsiderable and of so small consequence as not to deserve the attestation of miracles, so that there is no reason to expect that God should interpose by a miracle to convince men of them.

> Nec Deus intersit, nisi dignus vindice nodus
> Inciderit.

But for such truths as are necessary to be known by us but are not sufficiently evident of themselves, nor capable of cogent evidence, especially to prejudiced and interested persons, God is pleased in this case many times to work miracles

for our conviction ; and they are a proper argument
to convince us of a thing that is either in itself
obscure and hard to be believed, or which we are
prejudiced against and hardly brought to believe,
for they are an argument *a maiore ad minus*, they
prove a thing which is obscure and hard to be
believed, by something that is more incredible,
which yet they cannot deny because they see it
done. Thus our Saviour proves himself to be an
extraordinary person by doing such things *as never
man did* ; he convinceth them that they ought to
believe what he said, because they saw him do those
things which were harder to be believed (if one had
not seen them) than what he said.—[iii. 396, 397.]

'Tis true, miracles are now ceased among
Christians, our religion being sufficiently established by those which were wrought at first ; and
now the greatest miracle in these latter ages is a
good man, a true and sincere Christian. But the
laws of Christianity are still the same ; and the
motives to a good life are the same ; and tho' the
miraculous gifts of the Spirit have left the world,
yet the sealing and sanctifying gifts of the Holy
Ghost do still remain. . . . The admirable piety
and virtue of the first Christians are still upon
record for our imitation. But, I know not how it
comes to pass, we choose rather lazily to admire

those patterns than vigorously to imitate them, as if the holiness of those times were also miraculous and not intended for the imitation of succeeding ages, as if it were impossible for us now to lead such lives as they did, as if heaven and earth, God and men and all things, were altered since that time, as if the Christian religion were now quite dispirited, and had lost all its vigour and force, and as if the Holy Spirit of God had to all intents and purposes forsaken the world and were retired to the Father. But our religion is still the same as it was, the precepts of it as reasonable and the promise of it as powerful as ever. God is still the same as he was, and Christ still at the right hand of God, *making intercession for us*, and the Holy Spirit of God still ready to assist us *to every good word and work.*—[iii. 480.]

MISSIONS

AMONG the many bad things that have been done in the church of Rome there is one good thing very much to their honour, that they have been at very great charge and pains in their missions for the conversion of infidel nations, especially in the eastern parts of the world, to that which they account the true Christian religion. And if the matter had been as honestly managed as I hope it was piously intended, and their charity and zeal had been equally warm for the conversion of the northern infidels, where there is nothing to be met with but frost and cold, as it hath been for the conversion of those parts of the world where gold and spices abound, it had deserved great praise, notwithstanding their mistakes in religion and the great mixture of errors and corruptions in it. And it is no small reproach to the Protestant religion that there hath not appeared an equal zeal among us for this purpose, and that, to our unwearied endeavours to promote the interests of trade in foreign parts, there hath not been joined a like zeal and industry for the propagating of the Christian religion—which surely might be attempted, with more than ordinary advantage, in those places where we have so free a commerce. It is not good for men to be confident where they are not certain ; but it seems to me not improbable, if the conversion of infidels to Christianity were sincerely and vigorously attempted by men of honest minds, who would make it their business to instruct these who are strangers to our religion in the pure doctrine of Christianity, free from all human mixtures and corruptions, it seems to me in this case not at all improbable that God would extraordinarily countenance such an attempt by all fitting assistance, as he did the first publication of the gospel. For, as the wisdom of God is not wont to do that which is superfluous, so neither is it wanting in that which is necessary.—[iii. 274.]

I do strongly hope that there still remains a great harvest among the Gentiles yet to be gain'd to Christianity before the end of the world, and that the providence of God will, in his own appointed time, make a further step in the conversion of infidel nations, and that more of the kingdoms of the earth shall become the kingdoms of the Lord and of his Christ, and that yet before the end of all things the light of the gospel shall be displayed in a glorious manner not only in those vast regions of Tartary and China and Japan and Indostan, and other great kingdoms of the East, but in the large and dark regions of the new discovered world.—[iii. 247.]

MOTHERS SHOULD NURSE THEIR BABES

THE pains of nursing as well as of bearing children do insensibly create a strange tenderness of affection and care in the mother. *Can a woman*, says God, *forget her sucking child, that she should not have compassion on the son of her womb? Can a woman?*—that is, a mother, not a nurse, for the sucking child is said to be *the son of her womb*. . . . This affection and tenderness Nature, which is our surest guide and director, hath implanted in all living creatures towards their young ones ; and there cannot be a greater reproach to creatures that are endued with reason than to neglect a duty to which Nature directs even the brute creatures by a blind and unthinking instinct. So that it is such a duty as cannot be neglected without a downright affront to Nature, and from which nothing can excuse but disability or sickness or the evident danger of the mother or the inter-position of the father's authority, or some very extraordinary and public necessity.

This, I foresee, will seem a very hard saying to nice and delicate mothers, who prefer their own ease and pleasure to the fruit of their own bodies. But whether they will hear or whether they will forbear, I think myself obliged to deal plainly in this matter, and to be so faithful as to tell them that this is a natural duty, and, because it is so, of a more necessary and indispensable obligation than any positive precept of revealed religion,[1]

[1] An exaggeration, of course ; preachers sometimes fall into these strained statements. But it rises out of Tillotson's general belief about natural virtues.

and that the general neglect of it is one of the great and crying sins of this age and nation. . . .

There are two objections which indeed are real, but yet seem to have too much weight with those who would fain decline this duty, and are by no means sufficient to excuse mothers, no, not those of the highest rank and quality, from the natural obligation of it. And they are these : the manifest trouble and the manifold restraints which the careful discharge of this duty does unavoidably bring upon those who submit themselves to it. First, for the trouble of it, I have only this to say, and I think that no more needs to be said about it : that nobody is discharged from any duty by reason of the trouble which necessarily attends it, and is inseparable from it, since God who made it a duty foresaw the trouble of it when he made it so. Secondly, as to the manifold restraints which it lays upon mothers. This duty restrains mothers from spending their morning and their money in curious and costly dressing, from mis-spending the rest of the day in formal and for the most part impertinent [irrelevant] visits, and in seeing and hearing plays, many of which are neither fit to be seen or heard by modest persons and those who pretend to religion and virtue—as I hope all Christians do, especially persons of higher rank and quality ; and it restrains them likewise from trifling away a great part of the night in gaming and in revelling till past midnight (I am loth to say how much).

These are those terrible restraints which this natural duty of mothers nursing their children lays upon them. Now I cannot but think all these to be very happy restraints—happy surely for the child, and in many respects happy for the father and for the whole family, which by this means will be kept in much better order, but happiest of all for the mother, who does herein not only discharge a great and necessary duty, but is hereby also hindered from running into many great faults, which, before they will be forgiven, must cost her a deep contrition and a very bitter repentance.

Perhaps I may have gone farther in this unusual argument than will please the present age, but I hope posterity will be so wise as to consider it and lay it to heart. For I am greatly afraid that the world will never be much better till this great fault be mended.—[i. 488-490.]

OBJECTIONS TO JESUS

THE most unreasonable prejudice of all, in respect of his extraction, was grounded upon a spiteful and malicious proverb concerning the country where our Saviour was brought up and they supposed him to be born ; and that was Galilee (John i. 46, *Can any good thing come out of Nazareth ?* and John vii. 41, *Shall the messias come out of Galilee ?* and *v.* 52, *Search and look, for out of Galilee ariseth no prophet*). But it seems Nathanael, who was a good man, was easily taken off from this common prejudice when Philip said to him, *Come and see.* He bids him come and see the works he did, and then refers to him whether he would believe his own eyes or an old proverb. However, it seems the Jews laid great weight upon it, as if this alone were enough to confute all his miracles ; and after they had shot this bolt at him, the business was concluded clearly against him ! But prudent and considerate [thoughtful] men do not use to give much credit to ill-natured proverbs ; the good or bad characters which are given of countries are not understood to be universally true and without exception. There is no place but hath brought forth some brave spirits and excellent persons, whatever the general temper and disposition of the inhabitants may be. Among the Grecians, the Bœotians were esteemed a dull people, even to a proverb ; and yet Pindar, one of their chief poets, was one of them. The Scythians were a barbarous nation, and one would have thought no good could have come from thence ; and yet that country yielded Anacharsis, the eminent philosopher. The Idumeans were aliens and strangers to the covenant; and yet Job, one of the best men that ever was, came from thence. God can raise up eminent persons from any place— Abraham from Ur of the Chaldees and an idolatrous people! Nay, as our Saviour tells us, he can *out of these stones raise up children unto Abraham.* The Wise God, in the government of the world, does not tie himself to our foolish proverbs. It is not necessary, to make a man a prophet, that he should be bred in a good one. If God sends such a man, it matters not from what place he comes.— [ii. 401, 402.]

As to the time of our Saviour's appearance, it is objected that, if he be the only way and means of salvation, why did he come no sooner into the world, but suffer mankind so long without any hopes or means of being saved? This was objected by Porphyry of old, and still sticks in the minds of men. To this I answer: (1) It is not fit for creatures to call their Creator to too strict an account of his actions. Goodness is free, and may act when and how it pleaseth; and as *God will have mercy on whom he will have mercy*, so he may have mercy at what time he pleaseth, and is not bound to give us an account of his matters. . . . God took his own time, and he best knew what time was fittest. The

Scripture tells us that *in the fulness of the time God sent his Son,* when things were ripe for it, and all things accomplished that God thought requisite in order to it. In judging of the actions of our earthly governors, those who are at a distance from their counsels, what conjectures soever they may make of the reasons of them, will nevertheless, if they have that respect for their wisdom which they ought, believe that, how strange soever some of their actions may seem, yet they were done upon good reason, and that they themselves, if they knew the secrets of their counsels, should think so. Much more do we owe that reverence to the infinite wisdom of God, to believe that the counsels of his will are grounded upon very good reason, tho' we do not see many times what it is. (2) It is not true that the world was wholly destitute of a way or means of salvation before our Saviour's coming. Before the law of Moses was given, men were capable of being received to the mercy and favour of God, upon their obedience to the law of nature, and their sincere repentance for the violation of it, by virtue of *the Lamb that was slain from the foundation of the world.* Men were saved by Christ both before and under the law, without any particular and express knowledge of him. There were good men in other nations as well as among the Jews, as Job and his friends also seem to have been. In all ages of the world and *in every nation they that feared God and wrought righteousness were accepted of him.* The sacrifice of Christ, which is the meritorious cause of the salvation of mankind, looks back as well as forward ; and God was reconcileable to men, and their sins were pardoned, by virtue of this great propitiation that was to be made. In which sense, perhaps, it is that Christ is said to be *the Lamb slain from the foundation of the world* ; the apostle intimates to us that if this sacrifice, which was offered in the last ages of the world, had not been available in former ages, *Christ must have suffered often since the foundation of the world ; but now he hath appeared once in the conclusion of the ages to put away sin by the sacrifice of himself.* . . .

This was likewise the fittest season for the easy diffusing and propagating of the Christian religion. The Romans, together with their conquests, did very much propagate their language, which made the ways of communication far more easy ; and by the long and frequent correspondence of the several parts of the empire one with another, the ways of travel and passage from one country to another were more ready and open. So that no age can be instanced in all respects so convenient for the speedy propagation of a new religion as that wherein our Saviour appeared, viz. when the Roman empire was at its height. And it was very agreeable to the goodness and wisdom of the divine providence that the bravest and most virtuous of people in the world (infinitely beyond either the Persians or Grecians) should be chosen by God as one of the chiefest means for the spreading of the best and most perfect revelation that ever God made to the world.—[ii. 407-409.]

It is further objected that he hath left to us no example of that which by many is esteemed the only religious state of life, viz. perfect retirement from the world, for the more devout serving of God and freeing us from the temptations of the world—such as is that of monks and hermits. This perhaps may seem to some a great oversight and omission. But our Lord in great wisdom thought fit to give a pattern of a quite different sort of life, which was, not to fly the conversation of [intercourse with] men and to live in a monastery or a wilderness, but to do good among men, to live in the world with great freedom and with great innocency. He did indeed sometimes retire himself for the more free and private exercise of devotion, as we ought to do ; but he passed his life chiefly in the conversation of men, that they might have all the benefit that was possible of his instruction and example. We read that *he was carried into the wilderness to be tempted,* but not that he lived there to avoid temptation. He hath given us an example of denying the world without leaving it.—[iii. 229.]

ON USING OUR OPPORTUNITIES

THE season of the continuance of these means of grace and salvation which are afforded to us is uncertain to us. We know not how long they may be vouchsafed to us, nor how soon they may be taken away from us. *Yet a little while the light is with you,* saith our Saviour to the Jews, meaning that he himself should shortly be put to death and removed from them. This is not just our case. But thus far it agrees, that the light of the gospel, and the blessed opportunities which thereby we enjoy, are of an uncertain continuance, and may be of a lesser or longer duration as God pleaseth, and according as we make use of them and demean ourselves under them. I remember a very odd passage [1] in Mr. Herbert's Poems, which, whether it be only the prudent conjecture and fore-

---

[1] These famous lines, in 'The Church Militant,' at least the first two of them, were resented by the Vice-Chancellor of Cambridge University, whose licence had to be secured before the Poems of Herbert could be printed after his death; they seemed to the censor an overt reflection upon the religious policy of England. Eventually he agreed to pass the offending passage, muttering, ' I hope the world will not take him to be an inspired prophet.'

sight of a wise man or there be something more prophetical in it, I cannot tell ; it is this :

> Religion stands on tiptoe in our land,
> Ready to pass to the American strand.
> When Seine shall swallow Tiber, and the Thames,
> By letting in them both, pollutes her streams . . .
> Then shall religion to America flee;
> They have their times of gospel, even as we.

The meaning of it is this, that when the vices of Italy shall pass into France, and the vices of both shall overspread England, then the gospel will leave these parts of the world and pass into America, to visit these dark regions which have so long *sat in darkness and the shadow of death.* And this is not so improbable, if we consider what vast colonies in this age have been transplanted out of Europe into those parts, as it were on purpose to prepare and make way for such a change. But however that may be, considering how impiety and all manner of wickedness do reign among us, we have too much cause to apprehend that, if we do not reform and grow better, the providence of God will find some way or other to deprive us of that light which is so abused and affronted by our wicked and lewd lives ; and God seems now to say to us, as our Lord did to the Jews, *Yet a little while the light is with you ; walk while ye have the light, lest darkness come upon you.*—[iii. 587.]

ORTHODOXY

MEN stand much upon the title of ' orthodox,' by which is usually understood, not believing the doctrine of Christ or his apostles but such opinions as are in vogue among such a party, such systems of divinity as have been compiled in haste by those whom we have in admiration ; and whatever is not consonant to these little bodies of divinity, tho' possible it agree well enough with the Word of God, is error and heresy ; and whoever maintains it can hardly pass for a Christian among some angry and perverse people. I do not intend to plead for any error, but I would not have Christianity chiefly measured by matters of opinion. I know no such error and heresy as a wicked life. That man believes the gospel best who lives most according to it. Tho' no man can have a worse opinion of the Socinian doctrine than I have, yet I had rather a man should deny the satisfaction of Christ than believe it and abuse it to the encouragement of sin. Of the two, I have more hopes of him that denies the divinity of Christ and lives otherwise soberly and righteously and godly in the world, than of the man who owns Christ to be the Son of God and lives like a child of the devil.—[iii. 470.]

PENITENCE

THO' the highest degree of our sorrow doth necessarily fall below the evil of the least sin, yet God requires that we should be more deeply affected with some sins than others. But what is the lowest degree which God requires in a true penitent, and will accept, as it is impossible for us to tell, so it is unprofitable for anybody to know. For no man can reasonably make this enquiry with any other design than that he may learn how he may come off with God upon the cheapest and easiest terms. Now there cannot be a worse sign that a man is not truly sensible of the great evil of sin than this, that he desires to be troubled for it as little as may be, and no longer than needs must.—[iii. 19.]

I beseech you by the mercies of God, that mercy which naturally leads to repentance, and which is long-suffering to usward, on purpose that we may not perish but come to repentance, which hath spared us so often and is not yet exhausted and tired out by our intolerable obstinacy and innumerable provocations, that mercy which moved the Son of God to become man, to live among us, and to die for us ; who now, as it were, speaks to us from the

Cross, extending his pierced hands and painful
[full of pain] arms to embrace us, and through the
gaping wounds of his side let us see the tender and
bleeding compassion of his heart.—[iii. 14, 15.]

Nothing surely is easier than to put some bad
construction upon the best things, and so slur
even repentance itself and almost dash it out of
countenance, by some bold and perhaps witty
saying about it. But oh that men were wise!
Oh that men were wise! that they understood and
would consider their latter end. Come, let us
neither trifle nor dissemble in this matter. Of all
things in the world, let us not make a mock of
repentance, that which must be our last sanctuary
and refuge, and which we must all come to, before
we die.—[i. 270.]

WHY CHRISTIANS PERSECUTE

IF men will give themselves up to be swayed by
self-love and self-conceit, to be governed by
any base or corrupt interest, to be blinded by prejudice and intoxicated by pride, to be transported
and hurried away by violent and furious passions,
no wonder if they mistake the nature and confound
the differences of things in the plainest and most

palpable cases ; no wonder if God give up persons of such corrupt minds *to strong delusions, to believe in lies.* . . . In these cases men may take the wrong way and yet believe themselves to be in the right. . . .

Of this we have a plain and full instance in the Scribes and Pharisees, the chief priests and rulers among the Jews, who, because *they sought the honour of men and not that which was from God, and loved the praise of men more than the praise of God,* because they were prejudiced against the meanness of our Saviour's birth and condition, and had upon false grounds (though, as they thought, upon the infalli-bility of tradition and of Scripture interpreted by tradition) entertained quite other notions of the Messias from what he was really to be, because they were proud and thought themselves too wise to learn of him, and because his doctrine of humility and self-denial did thwart their interest and bring down their authority and credit among the people —therefore they set themselves against him with all their might, opposing his doctrine and blasting his reputation and persecuting him to the death : and all this while did bear up themselves with a conceit of the antiquity and privileges of their church, and their profound knowledge in the laws of God, and a great external show of piety and devotion and an arrogant pretence and usurpation

of being the only church and people of God in the
world ; and by virtue of their advantages they
thought they might do anything, and that whosoever opposed the authority of so ancient and good
a church must needs be very bad men and deserve
to be proceeded against in the severest manner.
As if any pretence of piety could give a privilege
to do wickedly, and by how much the wiser and
holier any man took himself to be, he might do so
much the worse things !

There is another remarkable instance of this in
St. Paul, who out of a blind and spurious zeal for
the *traditions of his fathers,* persecuted the true
church of God by imprisonment or death and all
manner of cruelties ; and all this while he *verily
thought* he was in the right and that he *ought to do*
all *these things against the name of Jesus of Nazareth.*
And if God had not in a miraculous manner checked
him in his course and changed his mind, he would
have spent his whole life in that course of persecution and cruelty, and would (with Pope Paul iv.
upon his death-bed) have recommended the Inquisi-
tion (or, if he could have thought of anything more
severe) to the chief priests and rulers of the Jewish
church.

I will not trouble you with nearer instances,
though the Jewish church is not the only church
in the world that hath countenanced the destruction

and extirpation of those who differ from them as a piece of very acceptable service to God and meritorious of the pardon of their sins.—[ii. 184, 185.]

PRAYER

IF the end of prayer were only to give God to understand what we want, it were all one what language we prayed in, and whether we understood what we asked of him or not; but as long as the end of prayer is to testify the sense of our wants and of our dependence upon God for the supply of them, it is impossible that any man should in any tolerable propriety of speech be said to pray who does not understand what he asks; and the saying over of so many paternosters by one that does not understand the meaning of them is no more a prayer than the repeating over so many verses in Virgil.—[ii. 367.]

All trust in God and dependence upon his providence does imply that we join prayer and endeavour together, faith in God and a prudent and diligent use of means. If we lazily trust the providence of God and so *cast all our care upon him* as to take none at all ourselves, God will take no care of us. In vain do we importune and tire heaven with our

prayers to help us against our enemies and perse-
cutors, if we ourselves will do nothing for ourselves.—[ii. 283.]

PROVIDENCE

THE government of the world is a very curious
and complicate thing, and not to be tampered
with by every unskilful hand.   And therefore, as
an unskilful man, after he hath tampered a great
while with a watch, thinking to bring it into better
order, and is at last convinced that he can do no
good upon it, carries it to him that made it, to mend
it and put it in order, so must we do, after all our
care and anxiety about our own private concernments or the public state of things ; we must give
over governing the world, as a business past our
skill, as a province too hard and a knowledge too
wonderful for us, and leave it to him who made the
world, to govern it and take care of it.—[ii. 563,
564.]

One way, among many others, whereby the
providence of God doth often interpose to decide
the events of war, is by a remarkable change of
the seasons and weather in favour of one side ; as
by sending great snows or violent rains to hinder
the early motion and march of a powerful enemy,

to the disappointment and prejudice of some great
design, by remarkable winds and storms at sea to
prevent the conjunction of a powerful fleet, and by
governing all these for a long time together so
visibly to the advantage of one side as utterly to
defeat the well-laid design of the other. Of all
which, by the great mercy and goodness of God
to us, we have had happy experience in all our
late signal deliverances and victories.[1]

And here I cannot but take notice of a passage
to the purpose in the book of Job; which may
deserve our more attentive regard and consideration, because I take this book to be incomparably
the most ancient of all other, and much elder than
Moses—and yet it is written with as lively a sense
of the providence of God and as noble figures and
flights of eloquence as perhaps any book extant in
the world. The passage I mean is, where God, to
convince Job of his ignorance in the secrets of
nature and providence, poseth him with many
hard questions, and with this amongst the rest:
Hast thou entered then into the treasures of the snow?
Hast thou seen the treasures of the hail, which I have
reserved against the time of trouble, against the day

[1] This is from a sermon preached at Whitehall, a thanksgiving discourse
before the King and Queen, on October 27, 1692. The battle of the
Boyne had been fought and won, on July 1, 1690; Limerick had sur-
rendered in October 1691, and the defeat of the French fleet off La Hogue,
on May 19, 1692, had checked a Jacobite invasion.

of battle and war? The meaning of which is, that the providence of God doth sometimes interpose to determine the events of war by governing the seasons and the weather, and by making the snows and rains, *the winds and storms, to fulfil his word* and to execute his pleasure.—[i. 387.]

It is possible that sin for a while may go unpunished, nay triumph and prosper, and that virtue and innocence may not only be unrewarded but oppressed and despised and persecuted. And this may be reconcileable enough to the wisdom of God's providence and the justice of it, supposing the immortality of the soul and another state after this life, wherein all things shall be set straight and every man shall receive according to his works. But unless this be supposed, it is impossible to solve the justice of God's providence. Who will believe that the affairs of the world are administered by him who loves righteousness and hates all the workers of iniquity, who will not let the least service that is done to him pass unrewarded, nor on the other hand acquit the guilty and let sin go unpunished, which are the properties of justice—I say, who will believe this, that looks into the course of the world and sees with how little difference and distinction of good and bad the affairs of it are manag'd, that sees virtue discountenanced and despised, poor and destitute, afflicted and tormented, when wickedness is many times exalted to high places and makes a great noise and ruffle in the world? He that considers what hazard many times good men run, how for goodness' sake they venture and many times quit all the contentments and enjoyments of this life and submit to the greatest sufferings and calamities that human nature is capable of, while in the meantime prosperity is poured into the lap of the wicked and heaven seems to look pleasantly upon those who deal treacherously and to be silent whilst the wicked devours *the man that is more righteous than himself* : he that considers this and can, without supposing another life after this, pretend to vindicate the justice of these things, must be as blind as the fortune that governs them. Would not this be a perpetual stain and blemish upon the divine providence, that Abel, who offered *a better sacrifice than Cain,* and *had this testimony that he pleased God,* should have no other reward for it than but to be slain by his brother who had offended God by a slight and contemptuous offering? If there were no reward to be expected after this life, would not this have been a sad example to the world, to see one of the first men that served God acceptably thus rewarded? . . . If we believe the being of God (which I do all along take for granted in this argument), there 's no other way imaginable to solve the equity and justice of God's providence but upon this supposition, that there is another life after this. For to say that virtue is a sufficient and abundant reward for itself, tho' it have some truth in it, if we set aside those sufferings and miseries and calamities which virtue is frequently attended with in this life, yet if these be taken in, it is but a very jejune and dry speculation.—[iii. 114, 115.]

THE REALITY OF GOD

THAT there have been so many false gods devised, is rather an argument that there is a true one than that there is none. There would be no counterfeits but for the sake of something that is real. For tho' all pretenders seem to be what they really are not, yet they pretend to be something that really is. For to counterfeit is to put on the likeness and appearance of some real excellence. There would be no brass money, if there were not good and lawful money. Bristol stones [1] would not pretend to be diamonds, if there never had been any diamonds. Those ' idols ' in Henry the Seventh's time (as Sir Francis Bacon

[1] A local rock-crystal, highly valued as a jewel.

calls them), Lambert Symnel and Perken Warbeck,[1] had never been set up, if there had not once been a real Plantagenet and Duke of York. So the idols of the heathen, though they be set up in affront to the true God, yet they rather prove that there is one than the contrary.—[i. 16.]

THE REFORMATION

IT is without doubt a very great sin to despise the communion of the Church or to break off from it, so long as we can continue in it without sin. But if things should once come to that pass that we must either disobey God for company or stand alone in our obedience to him, we ought most certainly to obey God, whatever comes of it, and to profess the truth, whether anybody else will join us in that profession or not. And they who speak otherwise condemn the whole Reformation, and do in effect say that Martin Luther had done a very ill thing in breaking off from the church of Rome, if nobody else would have joined with him in that honest design. And yet, if it had been so, I hope God would have given him the grace and courage to have stood alone in so good and glorious a cause, and to have laid down his life for it.—[i. 478.]

[1] Simnel personated the Earl of Warwick, and Warbeck the Duke of York.

RELIGION

THE plain truth of the matter is : men had rather religion should be anything than what indeed it is, the thwarting and crossing of our vicious inclinations, the curing of our evil and corrupt affections, the due care and government of our unruly appetites and passions, the sincere endeavour and constant practice of all holiness and virtue in our lives ; and therefore they had much rather have something that might handsomely palliate and excuse their evil inclinations than extirpate and cut them up.

This hath been the way and folly of mankind in all ages, to defeat the great end and design of religion, and to thrust it by, by substituting something else in the place of it, which they hope may serve the turn as well, and which hath the appearance of as much devotion and respect, and perhaps of more cost and pains, than that which God requires of them.   Men have ever been apt thus to impose upon themselves, and to please themselves with a conceit of pleasing God full as well, or even better, by some other way than that which he hath pitched upon and appointed for them, not considering that *God is a great King*, and will be observed and obeyed by his creatures in his own way, and that obedience to what he commands is better and more acceptable to him than any other sacrifice that we can offer, that he has not required at our hands.—[iii. 341, 342.]

It is a great mistake, and of very pernicious consequence to the souls of men, to imagine that the gospel is all promises on God's part, and that our part is only to believe them and to rely upon God for the performance of them, and to be very confident that he will make them good, though we do nothing else but only believe that he will do so. That the Christian religion is only a declaration of God's goodwill to us, without any expectation of duty from us, this is an error which one could hardly think could ever enter into any who have the liberty to read the Bible and attend to what they read and find there. The three great promises of the gospel are all very expressly contained in our Saviour's first sermon upon the mount. There we find the promise of *blessedness* often repeated but never absolutely made, but upon certain conditions and plainly required on our part, as repentance, humility, righteousness, mercy, peaceableness, meekness, patience. *Forgiveness of sins* is likewise promised, but only to those who make a penitent acknowledgment of them and ask forgiveness for them, and are ready to grant that forgiveness to others which they beg of God for themselves. *The gift of God's Holy Spirit* is likewise there promised, but it is upon condition of our earnest and importunate prayer to God. The gospel is everywhere full of precepts, enjoining duty and obedience upon our part, as well as of promises on God's part, assuring blessings to us, nay, of terrible threatenings also if we disobey the precepts of the gospel.— [ii. 272.]

I have only this to say, that if men will play the fool and make religion more troublesome than God hath made it, I cannot help that ; and that it is a false representation of religion which some in this world have made, as if it did chiefly consist not in pleasing God but in displeasing ourselves and tormenting ourselves. This is not to paint religion like herself, but rather like one of the Furies, with nothing but whips and snakes about her.— [i. 108.]

I know very well that good men may and often do blemish the reputation of their piety by overacting some things in religion, by an indiscreet zeal about things wherein religion is not concerned, by an ungrateful austerity and sourness which religion doth not require, by little affectations and an imprudent ostentation of devotion.—[i. 44.]

Does not religion consist very much in the duties of God's worship, in the exercise of piety and devotion, in constant and frequent prayers to God, and in the celebration of his goodness by praise and thanksgiving, in reading and hearing and meditating upon God's word, in fasting and abstinence and keeping our bodies in subjection to our spirits, and in frequent receiving of the holy sacrament? To this I answer that . . . these exercises of piety and devotion are but the means of religion, and not the ultimate end and design of it. And it is to be feared there are many which think that if they do but serve God in their families and go to church and behave themselves there with devotion and reverence, and at certain seasons receive the sacrament, they are truly religious and very good Christians, when all the while . . . they are covetous and earthly-minded, and to serve their covetousness will strain a point of truth or justice, and hardly do an act of charity in their whole lives but what is extorted from them by mere importunity or some such urgent necessity, in point of decency and reputation, that for shame of the world they know not how to avoid it; when their passions are as fierce and ungoverned, their hearts as full of gall and bitterness, their tongues of slander and evil-speaking, their humours as proud and surly and censorious, as theirs can be who are openly profane and seem to neglect and despise all religion. And yet, because they serve God (as they call it) and make an external appearance of piety and devotion, are good churchmen, and attend upon the ordinances of God, they think they have discharged the whole business of religion admirably well, and are very good children of God, and in a state of great grace and favour with him !—[ii. 511, 512.]

In vain does any one pretend that he will be a martyr for his religion, when he will not rule an appetite nor restrain a lust nor subdue a passion nor cross his covetousness and ambition for the sake of it, and in hope of that eternal life which God that cannot lie hath promised. He that refuses to do the less is not like to do the greater. It is very improbable that a man will die for his religion, when he cannot be persuaded to live according to it. He that cannot take up a resolution to live a saint, hath a demonstration within himself that he is never like to die a martyr.—[ii. 159.]

NATIONAL RELIGION

IT is most apparent that of late years religion is very sensibly declined among us. The manners of men have almost been universally corrupted by a civil war. We should therefore all jointly endeavour to retrieve the ancient virtue of the nation, and to bring into fashion again that solid and substantial, that plain and unaffected piety (free from the extremes both of superstition and enthusiasm) which flourished in the age of our immediate forefathers. Which did not consist in idle talk but in real effects, in a sincere love of God and of our neighbour, in a pious devotion and reverence towards the Divine Majesty, and in the virtuous actions of a good life, in the denial of *ungodliness and worldly lusts and in living soberly and righteously and godly in this present world.* This were the true way to reconcile God to us, to stop the course of his judgments, and to bring down the blessings of heaven upon us. God hath now been pleased to settle us again in peace, both at home and abroad, and he hath put us once more into the hands of our own counsel. Life and death, blessing and cursing, prosperity and destruction, are before us. We may choose our own fortune, and if we be not wanting to ourselves we may under the influence of God's grace and assistance, which are never wanting to our sincere endeavours, become a happy and a prosperous people.—[i. 40.]

RELIGION, NATURAL AND REVEALED

ALL religion is either natural or revealed. Natural religion consists in the belief of a God and in right conceptions and apprehensions concerning him, and in a due reverence and observance of him, and in a ready and cheerful obedience to those laws which he hath imprinted upon our nature, and the sum of our obedience consists in our conformity to God and our endeavour to be like him. For supposing God to have made no external revelation of his mind to us, we have no other way to know his will but by considering his nature and our own. And if so, then he that resembles God most is like to understand him best, because he finds those perfections in some measure in himself which he contemplates in the divine nature ; and nothing gives a man so sure a notion of things as practice and experience. . . . As for revealed religion, the only design of that is to revive and improve the natural notions which we have of God ; and all our reasonings about divine revelation are necessarily gathered by our natural notions of religion.—[ii. 208.]

All revealed religion does suppose and take for granted the clear and undoubted principles and precepts of natural religion, and builds upon them. By natural religion I mean obedience to the natural law, and the performance of such duties as natural light, without any express and supernatural revelation, doth dictate to men. . . . These and such like are those which we call moral duties ; and they are of eternal obligation, because they do naturally oblige, without any particular and express revelation from God, And these are the foundation of revealed and instituted religion, and all revealed religion does suppose them and build upon them ; for all revelation from God supposeth us to be men, and alters nothing of those duties to which we were naturally obliged before. . . . The great design of the Christian religion is to restore and reinforce the practice of the natural law, or, which is all one, of moral duties.—[ii. 307, 309.]

The change which Christianity design'd was the least liable to exception that could be, being nothing else in the main of it but the reducing of natural religion, the bringing men back to such apprehensions of God and such a way of worshipping him as was most suitable to the divine nature and to the natural notions of men's minds, nothing else but a design to persuade men of the one true God, maker of the world, that he is a Spirit and to be worshipped in such a manner as is suitable to his spiritual nature. And then, for matters of practice, to bring men to the obedience of these precepts of temperance and justice and charity, which had been universally acknowledged even by the heathen themselves to be the great duties which men owe to themselves and others.—[ii. 405.]

REMEMBER GOD

REMEMBRANCE is the actual thought of what we do habitually know. To remember God is to have him actually in our minds, and upon all proper occasions to revive the thoughts of him. . . . And the course of a religious life is not unfitly expressed by our ' remembrance of God.' For to remember a person or thing is to call them to mind upon all proper and fitting occasions, to think actually of them, so as to do that which the remembrance of them does require or prompt us to. To remember a friend is to be ready upon occasion to do him all good offices. To remember a kindness and benefit is to be ready to acknowledge and requite it when there is an opportunity. To remember an injury is to be ready to revenge it. And, in a word, to remember anything is to be mindful to do that which the memory of such a thing doth naturally suggest to us.—[i. 515.]

THE SATIRICAL SPIRIT

SATIRE and invective are the easiest kind of wit. . . . Wit is a keen instrument, and every one can cut and gash with it, but to carve a beautiful image and to polish it, requires great art and dexterity. To praise anything well is an argument of much more wit than to abuse. A little wit and a great deal of ill-nature will furnish a man with satire, but the greatest instance of wit is to commend well. And perhaps the best things are the hardest to be duly commended. This I say on purpose to recommend to men a nobler exercise for their wits, and, if it be possible, to put them out of conceit with that scoffing humour which is so easy and so ill-natured and is not only an enemy to religion but to everything else that is wise and worthy. And I am very much mistaken if the State as well as the Church, the civil government as well as religion, do not in a short space find the intolerable inconvenience of this humour.— [i. 34.]

SIN

DO but consider a little what sin is. It is the shame and blemish of thy nature, the reproach and disgrace of thy understanding and reason, the great deformity and disease of thy soul, and the eternal enemy of thy rest and peace. It is thy shackles and thy fetters, the tyrant that oppresses thee and restrains thee of thy liberty and condemns thee to the basest slavery and the vilest drudgery. It is the unnatural and violent state of thy soul, the worm that perpetually gnaws thy conscience, the cause of all the evils and miseries, all the mischiefs and disorders, that are in the world ; it is the foundation and fuel of hell ; it is that which puts thee out of the possession and enjoyment of thyself, which doth alienate and separate thee from God, the fountain of bliss and happiness, which provokes him to be thine enemy, and lays thee open every moment to the fierce revenge of his justice, and, if thou dost persist and continue in it, will finally sink and oppress thee under the insupportable weight of his wrath, and make thee so weary of thyself that thou shalt wish a thousand times that thou hadst never been, and will render thee so perfectly miserable that thou wouldst esteem it a great happiness to exchange thy condition with the most wretched and forlorn person that ever lived upon earth, to be perpetually on a rack, and to lie down for ever under the rage of the most violent diseases and pains that ever afflicted mankind. Sin is all this which I have described, and will certainly bring upon thee all those evils and mischiefs which I have mentioned, and make thee far more miserable than I am able to express or thou to conceive. And art thou not yet resolved to leave it? Shall I need to use any other arguments to set thee against it, and to take thee off from the love and practice of it, than this representation which I have now made of the horrible nature and consequences of it?—[iii. 70.]

THE SIN OF ELI

WE must not use mildness in the case of a wilful and heinous sin, especially if it be exemplary and of public influence. To rebuke gently upon such an occasion is rather to countenance the fault, and seems to argue that we are not sensible enough of the enormity of it, and that we have not a due dislike and detestation for it. Such cold reproofs as those which old Eli gave his sons, *Why do you do such things? For I hear of your evil dealing by all this people*—that is, their carriage [conduct] was such as gave public scandal. *Nay, my sons, for it is not a good report that I hear; you make the Lord's people to transgress.* Such a cold reproof as this, when the crime was so great and notorious, was a kind of allowance of it,

and a partaking with them in their sin; and
so God threatens Eli with most terrible judgment
upon this very account, because *his sons made
themselves vile, and he restrained them not.*

So that our severity must be proportioned to the
crime. Where the fault is great, there greater
severity must be used—so much at least as may
be an effectual restraint for the future. Here was
Eli's miscarriage, that in the case of so great a fault
as his sons were guilty of, his proceeding was neither
proportioned to the crime nor to the end of reproof
and correction, which is amendment for the future,
but he used such mildness in his reproof of them as
was more apt to encourage them than restrain them
in their vile courses.

I know very well that this enormous wickedness
of Eli's sons was committed by them after they
were grown to be men; but this instance is nevertheless to my present purpose,[1] there being hardly
any doubt to be made but that it was the natural
effect of a remiss and too indulgent education.—
[i. 497, 498.]

[1] He is preaching upon the education of children.

SINCERITY IN SPEECH.[1]

THE old English plainness and sincerity, that generous integrity of nature and honesty of disposition, which always argues true greatness of mind, and is usually accompanied with undaunted courage and resolution, is in a great measure lost among us ; there hath been a long endeavour to transform us into foreign manners and fashions, and to bring us to a servile imitation of none of the best of our neighbours, in some of the worst of their qualities. The dialect of conversation is nowadays so swelled with vanity and compliment [2] and so surfeited (as I may say) with expressions of kindness and respect, that if a man that lived an age or two ago should return into the world again, he would really want a dictionary to help him to understand his own language, and to know the true intrinsic value of the phrases in fashion, and would hardly at first believe at what low a rate the

---

[1] From the last sermon Tillotson preached, on 29th July 1694, five months before his death. Steele praises it highly in the *Spectator* (28th June 1711, and 14th April 1712) as a sincere sermon on sincerity : ' I do not know that I ever read anything that pleased me more.' This is one of the passages he cites, as does Addison (*Spectator*, n. 557).

[2] This term, or (as it was originally spelt) ' complement,' according to Donne (in 1623) ' is now denizened and brought into familiar use amongst us, and for the most part in an ill sense.'

highest strains and expressions of kindness imaginable do commonly pass in current payment; and
when he should come to understand it, it would
be a great while before he could bring himself with
a good countenance and a good conscience to converse with men upon equal terms and in their own
way. And in truth it is hard to say whether it
should more provoke our contempt or our pity to
hear what solemn expressions of respect and kindness will pass between men, almost upon no occasion, how great honour and esteem they will declare
for one whom they perhaps never heard of or saw
before, and how entirely they are all on the sudden
devoted to his service and interest, for no reason,
how ' eternally obliged to him,' for no benefit, and
how extremely they will be concerned for him, yea
and afflicted too, for no cause. It is still a just
matter of complaint that sincerity and plainness
are out of fashion, and that our language is running
into a lie, that men have almost quite perverted the
use of speech and made words to signify nothing,
that the greatest part of the conversation of mankind and of their intercourse with one another is
little else but driving a trade of dissimulation.—
[ii. 6.]

SOCRATES AND OTHERS

NOT that I believe that all virtues of the heathen were counterfeit and destitute of an inward principle of goodness. God forbid that we should pass so hard a judgment upon these excellent men, Socrates and Epictetus and Antonius,[1] and several others, who sincerely endeavoured to live up to the light and law of Nature and took so much pains to cultivate and raise their minds, to govern and subdue the irregularity of their sensual appetites and brutish passions, to purify and refine their manners, and to excel in all virtue and goodness ! These were glorious lights in those dark times, and so much the better for being good under so many disadvantages as the ignorance and prejudice of their educations, the multitude of evil examples continually in their view, and the powerful temptation of the contrary customs and fashions of the generality of mankind. Nor were they wholly destitute of an inward principle of goodness, for tho' they had not that powerful grace and assistance of God's Holy Spirit which is promised and afforded to all sincere Christians (as neither had the Jews, who were the peculiar people of God and in covenant with him), yet it is very

---

[1] *i.e.* Marcus Aurelius.

credible [1] that such persons were under a special care and providence of God, and not wholly destitute of divine assistance, no more than Job and his friends, mentioned in the Old Testament, and Cornelius in the New, who surely were very good men and accepted of God, tho' they were Gentiles and *aliens from the commonwealth* of Israel and *strangers from the covenant of promise,* but yet not excluded from the blessing of the Messias, tho' they were ignorant of him, as many of the Jews likewise were, nor from the benefits of that great propitiation which *in the fulness of time* he was to make for the sins of the whole world.

So that there is no need so uncharitably to conclude (as some of the ancients have done, not all, nor the most ancient of them neither) that there were no good men among the heathen, and that the brightest of their virtues were counterfeit and only in show and appearance.—[iii. 347.]

THE SOUL

THE most plain and popular notion we can have of the soul is that it is something in us which we never saw, and which is the cause of

---

[1] Dryden thought the same; the preface to *Religio Laici*, written in 1682, shows how he reconciled this hope and faith with the Athanasian Creed. It was a debated point in seventeenth-century theology, but Tillotson followed the line taken by men like Lord Herbert of Cherbury, Richard Baxter, and many other liberal-minded Christians.

those effects which we find in ourselves ; it is the principle whereby we are conscious to ourselves that we perceive such and such objects, that we see or hear or perceive anything by any other sense ; it is that whereby we think and remember, whereby we reason about anything, and do freely choose and refuse such things as are presented to us.—[iii. 109.]

THE STAGE

WHAT I have said about immodest and unchaste words is of equal force against lascivious books and pictures and plays, all which do alike intrench upon natural modesty, and for that reason are equally forbidden and condemned by the Christian religion; and therefore it may suffice to have named them. I shall only speak a few words concerning plays, which, as they are ordered now among us, are a mighty reproach to the age and nation.

To speak against them in general may be thought too severe, and that which the present age cannot well brook, and would not perhaps be so just and reasonable, because it is very possible they might be so framed and governed by such rules as not only to be innocently diverting but instructing and useful, to put some vices and follies out of countenance which cannot perhaps be so decently reproved nor so effectually exposed and corrected any other way.   But, as the stage now is, they are intolerable, and not to be permitted in a civilised, much less in a Christian, nation.   They do most notoriously minister both to infidelity and vice. By the performance of them they are apt to instil bad principles into the minds of men, and to lessen the awe and reverence which all men ought to have for God and religion ; and by their lewdness they teach vice and are apt to infect the minds of men and dispose them to lewd and dissolute practices. And therefore I do not see how any person pretending to sobriety and virtue, and especially to the pure and holy religion of our blessed Saviour, can without great guilt and open contradiction to his holy profession be present at such lewd and immodest plays, much less frequent them, as too many do, who yet would take it very ill to be shut out of the communion of Christians, as they would most certainly have been in the first and purest ages of Christianity.[1]—[iii. 383.]

---

[1] Tillotson, it must be remembered, was living during the period of the Restoration drama, of which critics who are no Puritans have said hard things.   Meredith, in his *Essay on Comedy*, observes that ' the men and women who sat through the acting of Wycherley's *Country Wife* were past blushing,' and that it is ' unjust to forget ' that Puritanism ' had once good reason to hate, shun, and rebuke our public shows.'   Macaulay's severe verdict on Dryden's dramas was that ' we are in a world where there is no veracity, no sense of shame, no humanity—a world for which any good-natured man would gladly take in exchange the society of Milton's devils.'

TIME WASTED

TIME is the season and opportunity of carrying on any work, and for that reason is one of the most valuable things.   And yet nothing is more wastefully spent and more prodigally squandered away by a great part of mankind than this, which, next to our immortal souls, is of all things most precious, because on the right use or abuse of our time our eternal happiness or misery does depend. Men have generally some guard upon themselves, as to their money and estates, and will not with open eyes suffer others to rob and deprive them of it.   But we will let almost anybody rob us of our time, and are contented to expose this precious treasure to everybody's rapine and extortion, and can quietly look on whilst men thrust in their hands and take it out by whole handfuls, as if it were of no greater value than silver was in Solomon's days, no more than *stones in the street*.   And yet, when it is gone, all the silver and gold in the world cannot purchase and fetch back the least moment of it, when perhaps we would give all the world for a very small part of that time which we parted with upon such cheap and easy terms. Good God, what a stupid and senseless prodigality is this ! Do we consider what we do when we give away such large portions of our time to our ease and pleasure, to diversion and idleness, or trifling and unprofitable conversation, to the making and receiving of impertinent [irrelevant] visits, and the usual and almost inseparable attendants thereof, spiteful observations upon them that are present and slandering and backbiting those that are absent (for the great design of most people in visits is not to better one another but to spy and make faults, and not to mend them, to get time off their hands, to show their fine clothes, and to recommend themselves to the mutual contempt of one another by a plentiful impertinence) ?—[ii. 292, 293.]

UNITY

ARE we not all members of the same Body and partakers of the same Spirit and heirs of the same blessed hope of eternal life ? So that, being brethren upon so many accounts, and by so many bonds and endearments all united one to another, and all travelling toward the same heavenly country, why do we *fall out by the way, since we be brethren* ? Why do we not, as becomes brethren, dwell together in unity, but are so apt to quarrel and break out into heats, to crumble into sects and parties, to divide and separate from one another upon every slight and trifling occasion ? Give me leave a little more fully to expostulate this matter, but very calmly and in the spirit of meekness, and in the name of our dear Lord who loved us at such a rate as to die for us, to recommend to you this *new commandment* of his, that ye *love one another*. Which is almost a *new commandment* still, and hardly the worse for wearing, so seldom is it put on, and so little hath it been practised among Christians for several ages ! Consider seriously with yourselves, ought not the great matters wherein we are agreed, our union in the doctrines of the Christian religion and in all the necessary articles of that *faith which was once delivered to the saints*, in the same sacrament, and in all the substantial parts of God's worship, and in the great duties and virtues of the Christian life, to be of greater force to unite us than differences in doubtful opinions and in little rites and circumstances of worship to divide and break us ?—[i. 174.]

THE WILL FOR THE DEED ?

HOW innocently soever it was intended, it is certainly a great mistake in divinity, and of a very dangerous consequence to the souls of men, to affirm that a desire of grace is grace, and conse-

quently by the same reason that a desire of obedience is obedience. A sincere desire and resolution
to be good is indeed a good beginning, and ought
by all means to be cherished and encouraged ; but
yet it is far from being the thing desired or from
being accepted for it in the esteem of God. For
God never accepts the desire for the deed, but where
there is no possibility, no opportunity, of doing the
thing desired. But if there be, and the thing be
not done, there is no reason to imagine that the
desire in that case should be accepted as if the
thing were done.—[i. 127.]

WISDOM

MEN do frequently murmur and repine at the
unequal distribution of other things, as
of health and strength, of power and riches ; but
if we will trust the judgment of most men concerning themselves, nothing is more equally shared
among mankind than a good degree of wisdom and
understanding. Many will grant others to be
superior to them in other gifts of nature, as in
bodily strength and stature, and in the gifts of
fortune, as in honour and riches, because the difference between one man and another in these qualities
is many times so gross and palpable that nobody

hath the face to deny it ; but very few in compari-
son, unless it be in mere compliment and civility,
will yield others to be wiser than themselves. And
yet the difference in this also is for the most part
very visible to everybody but themselves.—[i. 385.]

Happy are they that have it ; and, next to them,
not those many that think they have it, but those
few that know they have it not.—[i. 385.]

YOUTH

BESIDES the spirit and vigour of youth, young
persons have several other qualities which
make them very capable of learning anything that
is good. They are apt to believe, because they have
not been often deceived ; and this is a very good
quality in a learner. And they are full of hopes,
which will encourage them to attempt things even
beyond their strength, because hope is always of
the future, and the life of young persons is in a great
measure before them and yet to come. And, which
is a good bridle to restrain them from that which
is evil, they are commonly very modest and bashful.
And, which is also a singular advantage, they are
more apt to do that which is honest and commendable than that which is gainful and profitable,

being in a great measure free from *the love of money,*
which experience as well as the apostle tells us *is
the root of all evil.*   Children are seldom very
covetous, because they have seldom been bitten
by want.—[i. 519.]

ZEAL NOT ACCORDING TO KNOWLEDGE

HE that declares zealously for a party or opinion,
and is fierce and eager against those that
oppose it, seldom fails to gain the reputation of a
religious and godly man, because he hath the vote
of the whole party and a great number to cry him
up.   And if he be guilty of any miscarriage, unless
it be very gross and visible, he shall never want
those who will apologise for him and be ready to
vindicate him at all turns.   Either they will not
believe what is reported of him but impute it to
malice, or they will extenuate it and ascribe it to
human infirmity ; but still they cannot but think
he is a religious man, because he is so zealous for
that which they esteem to be so considerable a part
of religion.   Nay, such is the horrible partiality and
injustice of parties, that a very bad man, that
appears zealous for their way, shall easily gain the
esteem of a holy and religious man, though he have
many visible and notorious faults, though he be

passionate and ill-natured, censorious and un-charitable, cruel and oppressive, sordid and covet-ous ; when another who quietly and without any noise and bustle minds the substantial parts of religion and is truly devoted to God, just and peaceable and charitable towards men, meek and humble and patient, kind and friendly even to those that differ from him, shall hardly escape being censured for a lukewarm, formal, moral man, destitute of the grace of God and of the power of godliness.—[iii. 318.]

St. Mark hath it : *Go ye into all the world and preach the gospel to every creature* (xvi. 15). From which text, I suppose, St. Francis thought himself bound to preach to beasts and birds, and accord-ingly did it very often and with wonderful success, as they tell us in the legend of his life. But to extend our Saviour's commission so far, is want of common sense, in which St. Francis (tho' they tell us he had other gifts and graces to an eminent degree) was plainly deficient.—[ii. 451.]

What can be imagined more foolish and fanatical than St. Francis's stripping himself of his clothes and running about naked, than his frequent preach-ing to the birds and beasts and fishes ? Was ever anything more nauseously ridiculous than his picking up the lice which were beaten off his clothes and putting them in his bosom ? Which is magnified in him as a profound piece of humility, as if nastiness were a Christian grace. These and many other more such freaks which are related in his life as instances of his great sanctity serve to no other purpose but to render religion ridiculous to any man of common sense.—[iii. 518.]

How devout soever the woman might be, yet I dare say she was not over-wise and considerate [thoughtful], who, going about with a pitcher of water in one hand and a pan of coals in the other, and being asked what she intended to do with them, answered that she intended with the one to burn up heaven and with the other to quench hell, that men might love God and virtue for their own sakes, without hope of reward or fear of punishment.— [iii. 116.]

II. PASSAGES OF EXPOSITION

GENESIS iii. 12 : *The woman whom thou gavest to be with me, she gave me of the tree, and I did eat.*

MEN are very glad to lay their faults upon God, because he is a full and sufficient excuse, nothing being to be blamed that comes from him. This Adam did, upon the commission of the very first sin that mankind was guilty of. When God charged him for breaking of his law by eating of the fruit of the forbidden tree, he endeavoured to excuse himself by laying the fault obliquely upon God ; *the woman whom thou gavest to be with me, she gave me of the tree, and I did eat. The woman whom thou gavest to be with me*—he does what he can to derive the fault upon God. And tho' this be very unreasonable, yet it seems it is very natural. Men would fain have the pleasure of committing sin, but then they would be glad to remove as much of the guilt and trouble of it from themselves as they can.

GENESIS iv. 8 : *Cain rose up against Abel his brother and slew him.*

IT is said of Abel that God was pleased with his sacrifice, tho' with Cain's he was not well pleased. Upon this Cain was angry at his brother and slew him. Now, if the immortality of the soul and a future state be not supposed and taken for granted in this story, this very passage is enough to cut the sinews and pluck up the roots of all religion. For if there were no rewards after this life, it were obvious for every man to argue from this story that it was a dangerous thing to please God, if this was all that Abel got by it, to be knock'd on the head by his brother who offended God.

GENESIS xxix. 20 : *And Jacob served seven years for Rachel, and they seemed unto him but a few days, for the love he had to her.*

NOTHING is difficult to love. It will make a man deny himself and cross his own inclinations to pleasure them whom he loves. It is a passion of strange power where it reigns, and will cause a man to submit to those things with delight which in other circumstances would seem grievous to him. Jacob served for Rachel seven years, and after that seven years more ; *and they seemed unto him but a few days, for the love he had to her.* Did but the love of God rule in our hearts, and had we as real an affection for him as some men have for their friends, there are no such difficulties in religion but what love would conquer, and the severest parts of it would become easy when they were once undertaken by a willing mind.

JOSHUA xxiv. 15 : *But as for me and my house, we will serve the Lord.*

JOSHUA here resolves that, if need were and things were brought to that pass, he would stand alone, or with very few adhering to him, in the profession and practice of the true religion. And this is not a mere suggestion of an impossible case, which can never happen ; for it may, and hath really and in fact happened in several ages and places of the world. There hath been a general apostasy of some great part of God's Church from the belief and profession of the true religion to idolatry and to damnable errors and heresies, and some good men have, upon the matter, stood alone in the profession of the true religion, in the midst of this general defection from it. . . . Thus in the height of popery Wickliffe appeared here in England, Hierome of Prague and John Hus in Germany and Bohemia. And in the beginning of the Reformation, when popery had quite overrun these western parts of the world and subdued her enemies on every side, and Antichrist sat secretly in the quiet possession of his kingdom, Luther arose, a bold and rough man, but a fit wedge to cleave in sunder so hard and knotty a block, and appeared stoutly against the gross errors and corruptions of the church of Rome, and for a long time stood alone, and with a most invincible spirit and courage maintained his ground and resisted the united malice and force of Antichrist and his adherents, and gave him so terrible a wound that he is not yet perfectly healed and recovered of it.

2 SAMUEL iii. 39: *The sons of Zeruiah be too hard for me.*

IMPIETY and vice do strangely lessen greatness, and do secretly and unavoidably derive some weakness upon authority itself. Of this the Scripture gives us a remarkable instance in David. For among other things which made the sons of Zeruiah *too hard* for him, this probably was none of the least, that they were particularly conscious [privy] to his crimes.

2 SAMUEL xvi. 10 : *Let him curse, because the Lord hath said unto him, Curse David.*

THIS likewise should keep us from fretting and vexing at instruments and second causes, to consider that the wise providence of God over-ruleth and disposeth the actions of men, and that no harm can happen to us without his permission. This consideration restrained David's anger under that high provocation of Shimei, when he followed him, reproaching him and cursing him ; *Let him alone; the Lord hath said unto him, Curse David.* He considered that God's providence permitted it, and, looking upon it as coming from a higher hand, this calmed his passion.

NEHEMIAH v. 17-19 : *Moreover, there were at my table an hundred and fifty of the Jews and rulers, beside those that came unto us from among the heathen that are about us. Now that which was prepared for me daily was one ox and six choice sheep ; also fowls were prepared for me, and once in ten days store of all sorts of wine : yet for all this required not I the bread of the governor, because the bondage was heavy upon this people. Think upon me, my God, for good, according to all that I have done for this people.*

ONE would be apt to wonder that Nehemiah should reckon a huge bill of fare and a vast number of promiscuous guests amongst his virtues and good deeds, for which he desires God to remember him. But, upon better consideration, besides the bounty and sometimes charity of a great table (provided there be nothing of vanity or ostentation in it), there may be exercised two very considerable virtues; one is temperance, and the other is self-denial, in a man's being contented, for the sake of the public, to deny himself so much as to sit down every day to a feast, and to eat continually in a crowd, and almost never to be alone, especially when, as it often happens, a great part of the company that a man must have is the company that a man would not have.

PSALM ii. 8 : *Ask of me, and I shall give thee the heathen for thine inheritance, and the uttermost parts of the earth for thy possession.*

THAT solemn promise which God made to his Son, *Ask of me, and I will give thee the heathen for thine inheritance, and the utmost parts of the earth for thy possession,* seems to be very far from being yet fully accomplished, and, since this is like to be the work of some ages, the time perhaps is not far off when it shall begin. And tho' I see no sufficient grounds from Scripture to believe the personal reign of Christ upon earth for a thousand years, yet it seems to be not improbable that, some time before the end of the world, the glorious kingdom of Christ, I mean, the prevalency of the pure Christian religion, should be of as long continuance as the reign of Mahomet and Antichrist has been, both of which have now lasted about a thousand years.

PSALM xiv. 1 : *The fool hath said in his heart, There is no God. They are corrupt, they have done abominable works.*

WHEN men are *corrupt* and *do abominable works*, they *say in their hearts, There is no God.* That is, they would fain think so. And everything serves for an argument to a willing mind, and every little objection appears strong and considerable which makes against that which men are loth should be true.

PROVERBS xv. 8 : *The sacrifice of the wicked is an abomination to the Lord, but the prayer of the upright is his delight.*

IF we go on in our sins, our very prayers will become sin and increase our guilt. For *the prayer of the wicked* (that is, of one that is resolved

to continue so) *is an abomination to the Lord.*   Can
we think it reasonable for men to address themselves to God after this manner ?   ' Lord, though
we have no mind to turn to thee, yet we pray thee
turn away thine anger from us ;   though we are
resolved not to forsake our sins, yet we make no
doubt but thy mercy will forgive them ;   give peace
in our time, O Lord, that we may pursue our lusts
securely and without disturbance ;   deliver us from
the hands of our enemies, that we may sin against
thee without fear all the days of our life.'   Would
it not be horrible impudence and impiety to put
any such petitions to God ?   And yet this, I fear, is
the most genuine interpretation of our prayers and
lives compared together.

PROVERBS xxii. 6 : *Train up a child in the way he
     should go ; and when he is old, he will not depart
     from it.*

HERE is the consequent fruit and benefit of
     good education ; *and when he is old, he will
not depart from it.*   This we are to understand
according to the moral probability of things, not as
if this happy effect did always and infallibly follow
upon the good education of a child, but that this
very frequently is, and may probably be presumed
and hoped to be, the fruit and effect of a pious

and prudent education. Solomon means that from the very nature of the thing this is the most hopeful and likely way to train up a child to be a good man.

ECCLESIASTES vii. 11 : *Wisdom is good with an inheritance.*

GOOD education is the very best inheritance that you can leave to your children. It is a wise saying of Solomon that *wisdom is good with an inheritance*; but surely an inheritance without wisdom and virtue to manage it, is a very pernicious thing. And yet how many parents are there who omit no care and industry to get an estate that they may leave it to their children, but use no means to form their minds and manners for the right use and enjoyment of it, without which it had been much happier for them to have been left in great poverty and straits.

ECCLESIASTES xii. 1 : *Remember now thy Creator in the days of thy youth.*

WE are not so to remember our Redeemer as to forget our Creator. The goodness and power and wisdom of God, which appears in the creation of the world, ought still to be matter of admiration and praise to Christians.   It is a great fault and neglect among Christians that they are not more taken up with the works of God and the contemplation of the wisdom which shines forth in them.

Remember thy Creator, that is, honour, fear, love, obey, and serve him, and, in a word, do everything as becomes one that is mindful of God and hath him continually in his thoughts.   Consider that, notwithstanding the great obligation which lies upon us to *remember our Creator in the days of our youth*, we are most apt at that time of all others to forget him.   For that which is the great blessing of youth is also the great danger of it, I mean the health and prosperity of it ; and though men have then best reason, yet they are most apt to forget God in the height of pleasure and in the abundance of all things.

JEREMIAH vi. 15 : *Were they ashamed when they had committed abomination ?   Nay, they were not at all ashamed, neither could they blush.*

*W*ERE *they ashamed* (saith the prophet) *when they committed abomination ?   Nay, they were not ashamed, neither could they blush.*   When men have the heart to do a very bad thing, they seldom want the face to bear it out.

JEREMIAH xvii. 9 : *The heart is deceitful above all things, and desperately wicked : who can know it ?*

IT is indeed said in Scripture that *the heart is deceitful above all things, and desperately wicked : who can know it ?* Which is true, concerning our future intentions and actions. But though this be true in itself, yet 'tis not the meaning of that text. For the prophet in that chapter plainly makes use of this consideration of the falsehood and deceitfulness of man's heart as an argument to take off the people of Israel from *trusting in the arm of flesh,* and in these promises which are made to them of foreign assistance from Egypt, because men may pretend fair and yet deceive those that rely upon them— for *the heart of man is deceitful, and desperately wicked,* and none but God knows whether men's inward intentions be answerable to their outward professions. And this, I verily believe, is all that the prophet here intends : that there is a great deal of fraud and deceit in the hearts of bad men, so that no man can rely upon their promises and professions, but God knoweth the hearts of all men.

MICAH vi. 9 : *Hear ye the rod, and who hath ap-*
pointed it.

'TIS the advice of the prophet, *Hear ye the rod,*
and him that hath appointed it. Every rod
of God, every affliction, hath a voice, which doth
not only speak to the sufferers but to the spectators,
not only to those who are smitten but to those who
stand by and look on ; and if, when God sends
judgments upon others, we do not take warning
and example by them, if instead of reflecting upon
ourselves and trying our ways we fall a-censuring
of others, if we will pervert the meaning of God's
providences and will not understand the design and
intention of them, then we leave God no other way
to awaken us and to bring us to a consideration of
our evil ways but by pouring down his wrath upon
our heads, that so he may convince us to be sinners
by the same argument from whence we have concluded others to be so.

MATTHEW v. 16 : *Let your light so shine before men,*
that they may see your good works, and glorify
your Father which is in heaven.

RELIGION is not an invisible thing, consisting
in mere belief, in height of speculation and
niceties of opinion, or in abstruseness of mystery.

The Scripture does not place it in things remote
from the sight and observation of men, but in real
and visible effects, such as may be plainly dis-
cerned and even felt in the conversation of
men, not in abstracted notions but in substantial virtues and in a sensible power and efficacy
upon the lives of men, in all the instances of piety
and virtue, of holy and excellent actions.   This
our Saviour requires of his disciples, that the
virtue and holiness of their lives should be so
visible and conspicuous that all men may behold
it and give testimony to it and glorify God upon
that account.

MATTHEW vi. 33 : *Seek ye first the kingdom of God,
and his righteousness; and all these things shall
be added unto you.*

I T is a mighty encouragement to us to consider
that if we sincerely *seek the kingdom of God and
his righteousness*, there is not only a fair probability
of obtaining them, but all the security we can desire.
Men may be in good earnest for the things of this
world, may love them with all their hearts and souls
(as we see too many do) and seek them with all
their might and strength, and yet, after all, their
endeavours may be shamefully frustrated and dis-

appointed of their end.   There are many examples of this kind daily before our eyes, and yet men are not discouraged from seeking these things.   A fair probability, nay almost a possibility, of attaining them is enough to a worldly-minded man to drudge and toil for them.   Why, the same affection, the same zeal, the same unwearied endeavour to please God and to save our souls would infallibly bring us to heaven.   It was a sad but true saying of Cardinal Wolsey, when he was leaving the world, ' Had I been but as careful to please God as I have been to serve my prince, he would not have forsaken me now in the time of my grey hairs.'   Nay, it is to be hoped that less diligence and care about the concernments of our souls and another life than many use about the things of this life will secure our eternal happiness, or else it is to be feared that but very few would be saved.

MATTHEW x. 16, and EPHESIANS iv. 26.

THERE are two precepts in the New Testament that seem to me to be the nicest of all others and hardest to be put in practice.   One is that of our blessed Saviour : *be wise as serpents, and innocent as doves.*   How hard is it to hit upon the just temper of wisdom and innocency, to be wise and hurt nobody, to be innocent without being silly ! The other is that of the apostle : *be ye angry, and sin not.* How difficult too is this, never to be angry but upon just cause, and when the cause of our anger is just, not to be transported beyond due bounds, either as to the degree of our anger or as to the duration and continuance of it ! This is so very nice a matter that one would be almost tempted to think that this were in effect a prohibition of anger in any case : *be ye angry, and sin not*; be ye so, if ye can, without sin.

MATTHEW xvi. 26 : *What is a man profited, if he shall gain the whole world, and lose his own soul ?*

THE market was never yet so high ; no sinner had ever yet so great a value for his immortal soul as to stand upon such terms. Alas ! infinitely less than *the whole world*, the gratifying of a vile lust or an unmanly passion, the smile or the frown of a great man, the fear of singularity and of displeasing the company—these and suchlike mean and pitiful considerations tempt thousands every day to make away themselves and to be undone for ever.

MATTHEW xxvii. 51 : *The earth did quake, and the rocks rent.*

WHEN the Son of God suffered, the rocks were rent in sunder. And shall not the consideration of those sufferings be effectual to break the most stony and obdurate heart ?

LUKE iv. 12 : *Thou shalt not tempt the Lord thy God.*

THE devil tempted our Saviour to tempt God by casting himself down from the pinnacle of the temple, in confidence that the angels would take care of him ; but our Saviour answers him, *It is written, Thou shalt not tempt the Lord thy God.* From which instance it appears that men are said to tempt God whenever they expect the protection of his providence in an unwarrantable way. God hath promised to take care of good men, but if they neglect themselves or willingly cast themselves into danger and expect his providence and protection, they do not trust God but tempt him.

Luke xii. 15 : *And he said unto them, Take heed, and beware of covetousness.*

OUR Saviour doubles the caution that we may double our care. It is a sin very apt to steal upon us and slyly to insinuate itself into us under the specious pretence of industry in our callings and a provident care of our families ; but, however it may be coloured over, it is a great evil, dangerous to ourselves and mischievous to the world.

Luke xiii. 24 : *Strive to enter in at the strait gate : for many, I say unto you, will seek to enter in, and shall not be able.*

SEEKING, here, in opposition to *striving*, is a faint and weak endeavour, which will not carry us through this narrow and difficult passage. And this is the reason why many miscarry, who make some attempts toward heaven ; they do not *strive*, they do not put forth any vigorous endeavours to get thither.

Luke xv. 17, 18 : *I perish with hunger. I will arise and go to my father.*

THE providence of God makes use of hunger and extreme necessity to bring home the prodigal. And by him our Saviour represents to us the temper of most sinners ; for till we have spent that stock of mercies which God hath given us, till we come to be pinched with want and are ready to faint, we are not apt to entertain thoughts of returning to our Father.

LUKE xviii. 8 : *When the Son of man cometh, shall he find faith on earth ?*

VICE and superstition and enthusiasm, which are the reigning diseases of Christendom, when they have run their course and finished their circle, do all naturally end in atheism. And then it will be time for the great Judge of the world to appear, and effectually to convince men of that which they would not be persuaded to believe by any other means. And of this our Saviour hath given us a terrible and fearful intimation, in that question of his, *When the Son of man comes, shall he find faith upon earth ?* Our Saviour hath not positively affirmed it. And God grant that we may not make it, and find it, true.

JOHN iii. 19, 20 : *This is the condemnation, that light is come into the world, and men loved darkness rather than light, because their deeds were evil.*

*For every one that doeth evil hateth the light,
neither cometh to the light, lest his deeds should
be reproved.*

MEN of dissolute lives cry down religion
because they would not be under the
restraints of it ; they are loth to be tied up by the
strict laws and rules of it : 'tis their interest more
than any reason they have against it which makes
them despise it. They hate it because they are
reproved by it. So our Saviour tells us that *men
love darkness rather than light, because their deeds
are evil.*

ACTS x. 38 : *Who went about doing good.*

HOW unwearied our blessed Saviour was in
doing good ! He made it his only business,
and spent his whole life in it. He was not only
ready to do good to those that came to him and
gave him opportunity for it and besought him to
do it, but went himself from one place to another
to seek out objects to exercise his charity upon.
He went to those who could not and to those who
would not come to him. . . . He was at everybody's beck and disposal to do them good. When
he was doing cures in one place, he was sent for to
another.

ACTS xx. 35 : *Remember the words of the Lord Jesus, how he said, It is more blessed to give than to receive.*

THIS was the life which God himself, when he was pleased to become man, thought fit to lead in the world, giving us herein an example that we should follow his steps. He made full trial and experience of the happiness of this temper and spirit, for he was all on the giving hand.

ROMANS iii. 8 : ' *Let us do evil, that good may come* ' —*whose damnation is just.*

ST. PAUL tells us that they who said they might do evil that good might come, *their damnation is just.* He tells us indeed that some would have charged this doctrine upon the Christians, and particularly upon himself ; but he rejects it with the greatest detestation, and (which is not unworthy of our observation) in his epistle to the Roman church, as if the Spirit of God, to whom all times are present, had particularly directed him to give this caution to this church, that in future ages they might be warned against so pernicious a principle and all wicked practices that are consequent upon it.

1 CORINTHIANS i. 20 : *Where is the disputer of this world ?*

I KNOW not whether St. Paul, who had been taken up into the third heaven, did by that question of his intend to insinuate that this wrangling work hath place only in this world and upon this earth, where only there is a dust to be raised, but will have no place in the other. But whether St. Paul intended this or not, the thing itself, I think, is true, that in the other world all things will be clear and past dispute. To be sure, among the blessed—and probably also among the miserable, unless fierce and furious contentions, with great heat without light, about things of no moment and concernment to them, should be designed for a part of their torment.

PHILIPPIANS ii. 7 : *Who made himself of no reputation.*

TO submit to contempt is to empty oneself indeed, reputation being one of the last things a generous mind would be content to forgo, and that which some have held in equal dearness and esteem with life itself ; yet in this our Lord denied himself, and, that he might do good to mankind, was contented to be esteemed one of the worst of men, and, without any kind of cause or desert, to undergo all manner of obloquy and reproach, to be accounted a magician and impostor, *a friend of publicans and sinners,* a seducer of the people, a seditious person, and more worthy of the most cruel and shameful death than the greatest malefactor. Thus was the Son of God contented to be set below the worst of men, to be abased and vilified, that he might be the perfect pattern to us of this difficult virtue of self-denial, even in those things which are held in the greatest esteem among the best of men.

HEBREWS xi. 24 : *By faith Moses, when he was come to years, refused to be called the son of Pharaoh's daughter.*

THIS was a deliberate choice, not any rash and sudden determination made by him when he was of incompetent age to make a true judgment of matters. And this the apostle takes notice of in the text as a very memorable circumstance, that, *when he was come to years, he refused to be called the son of Pharaoh's daughter.* And St. Stephen tells us (Acts vii. 23) that he was *full forty years old* when he made this choice.

JAMES i. 14 : *Every man is tempted, when he is drawn away of his own lust, and enticed.*

I AM far from thinking that the devil tempts men to all the evil that they do. I rather think that the greatest part of the wickedness that is committed in the world springs from the evil motions of men's own minds. Men's own lusts are generally to them the worst devil of the two, and do more strongly incline them to sin than any devil without them can tempt them to it. . . . And I wish that our own age did not afford us too many instances of this kind, of such forward and expert sinners as need no tempter either to excite or instruct them to that which is evil. Now in this case the devil betakes himself to other persons, and removes his snares and baits where he thinks there is more need and occasion for them.[1]

1 PETER iv. 11 : *If any man speak, let him speak as the oracles of God.*

WE must be serious in our instructions and exemplary in our lives. Serious in our instructions : this the apostle certainly requires in

---

[1] So Sir Thomas Browne writes in *Christian Morals* (i. 20) : ' Our corrupted hearts are the factories of the devil, which may be at work without his presence ; for when that circumventing spirit hath drawn malice, envy, and all unrighteousness unto well-rooted habits in his disciples, then iniquity goes on upon its own legs.'

the highest degree, when he chargeth ministers so to *speak as the oracles of God.* To which nothing can be more contrary than to trifle with the word of God and to speak of the weightiest matters in the world, the great and everlasting concernments of the souls of men, in so slight and indecent a manner as is not only beneath the gravity of the pulpit but even of a well-regulated stage. Can anything be more unsuitable than to hear a minister of God from this solemn place to break jests upon sin and to quibble upon the vices of the age ? This is to shoot without a bullet, as if we had no mind to do execution, but only to make men smile at the mention of their faults ; this is so nauseous a folly and of so pernicious consequence to religion, that hardly anything too severe can be said of it.

1 JOHN iii. 2 : *We shall see him as he is.*

WHAT is meant here by seeing God ? The schoolmen have spun out abundance of fine cobwebs about this, which in their language they call the beatific vision of God, and they generally describe and explain it so as to render it a very dry and sapless thing. . . . But surely the Scripture understands something more by the sight of God than a bare contemplation of him. To see a

friend is to enjoy the pleasure of his company and
the advantages of his conversation. So here, the
sight of God doth comprehend and take in all the
happiness of our future state. As to see the king
includes the court and all the glorious circumstances of his attendance, so to *see God* does take
in all that glory and joy and happiness which flows
from his presence.

JUDE 9 : *Michael the archangel, when contending
with the devil he disputed about the body of Moses,
durst not bring against him a railing accusation.*

HIS duty restrained him from it, and probably
his discretion too. As he durst not offend
God, in doing a thing so much beneath the dignity
and perfection of his nature, so he could not but
think that the devil would have been too hard for
him at railing—a thing to which, as the angels
have no disposition, so I believe that they have no
talent, no faculty at it. The cool consideration
whereof should make all men, especially those who
call themselves ' divines,' and especially in controversies about religion, ashamed and afraid of this
manner of disputing.

III. SAYINGS AND SENTENCES

I T should make our blood to rise in our faces, to consider what a distance there is between our religion and our lives.

WHEN all is done, there is no such error or heresy, nothing so fundamentally opposite to religion, as a wicked life.

WE have no cause to be ashamed of the gospel of Christ, but the gospel of Christ may justly be ashamed of us.

IT is by no means necessary to salvation to believe that St. Matthew wrote the history of the gospel, but only to believe what he wrote.

ALL religions are equal in this, that a bad man can be saved in none of them.

MEN *say* they believe this or that, but you may see in their lives what it is they believe.

HE that would know what a man believes, let him attend rather to what he does than to what he talks.

IT is a power which every man is naturally invested withal, to *consider* and *judge* and *choose* : to *consider*, that is, to weigh and compare things together, to *judge*, that is, to determine which is best, and to *choose*, that is, to resolve to do it or not.

TRUTH carries great evidence along with it, and is very convincing ; and where men will not yield to it and suffer themselves to be convinced by it, it gives them a great deal of disturbance.

A MAN may as soon be well without health as happy without goodness.

HE is truly charitable who would not only as soon but rather sooner give his alms in secret than in the sight of men. And he is truly grateful who, when there is occasion and opportunity, will acknowledge a kindness and requite a benefit to the relations of his deceased friend, though he be sure that all memory of the obligation died with him, and that none are conscious of it but God and his own conscience.

MY nature inclines me to be tender and compassionate ; a hearty zeal for our religion and concernment for the public welfare of my country may perhaps have made me a little severe ; but neither my natural disposition nor the temper of the English nation nor the genius of the Protestant, that is, the true Christian religion, will allow me to be cruel.

MANY are fit to be reproved, whom yet every man is not fit to reprove.

NEXT to a good conscience, a good reputation ought to be to every man the dearest thing in the world.

TRUTH never grows old, and those laws of goodness and righteousness which are contained in the gospel are still as reasonable and apt to gain upon the minds of men as ever.

THE soul of man is an active principle, and will be employed one way or other ; it will be doing something.

As it is pleasant to the eye to have an endless prospect, so it is some pleasure to a finite understanding to view unlimited excellences which have no shore or bounds, tho' it cannot comprehend them. There is a pleasure in admiration, and this is that which properly causeth admiration, when we discover a great deal in an object which we understand to be excellent, and yet we see we know not how much more beyond that, which our understandings cannot fully reach and comprehend.

THE wit of man doth more naturally vent itself in satire and censure than in praise and panegyric.

THERE are no kinds of sins lie heavier upon a man's conscience than those of injustice, because they are committed against the clearest natural light, and there's the least natural temptation to them.

THIS is the desperate folly of mankind, that they seldom think seriously of the consequences of their actions.

OUR ascent to heaven is steep and narrow, and we are safest when we do not stand still ; temptation cannot so well take its aim at us.

IT is a great way that we may go in a short time, if we be always moving and pressing forward.

GOD hath so contrived things that ordinarily

the pleasures of human life do consist more in hope than in enjoyment.

It is, I think, a true observation that catechising and the history of the martyrs have been the two great pillars of the Protestant religion.

It is a pity it should be so, but I am afraid it is too true that the greatest mischiefs that have been done to the world have been done by silly, well-meaning men.

There are some prejudices which cannot be plucked out of the minds of men at once, but yet may be so loosened by degrees that they will fall off by themselves ; as there are many knots untied with patience and leisure, which by a violent pulling are fixed so much the faster.

Whatever in religion is necessary to be known by all must in all reason be plain and easy and lie level to all capacities.

'Tis a sad presage of apostasy, to stand still in religion. He that once stops, the next thing is to look back.

'Tis a fond thing for a man to think to set bounds to himself in anything that is bad, to resolve that he will commit this sin and then give over, entertain but this one temptation and after that he will shut the door and admit of no more.

As there is a connexion of one virtue with another, so vices are link'd together, and one sin draws many after it.

GOD hath nowhere said that he will be merciful to those who, upon the score of his mercy, are bold with him and presume to offend him ; *but the mercy of the Lord is upon them that fear him and keep his covenant and remember his commandments to do them. There is forgiveness with him, that he may be feared,* but not that he may be despised and affronted. This is to contradict the very end of God's mercy, which is to *lead us to repentance,* to engage us to leave our sins, not to encourage us to continue in them.

I DO not believe that God hath absolutely predestinated any man to ruin, but by a long course of wilful sin men may in a sort predestinate themselves to it.

I AM horribly afraid it is too true that a sinner may arrive to that confirmed state of impiety as almost totally to lose his liberty to do better.

IT is now almost become natural to men, to supply the want of a good conscience by a good conceit of themselves.

WE distrust the providence of God, when, after we have used our best endeavours and begged his blessing upon them, we torment ourselves about the wise issue and event of them.

IT is a dangerous thing in divinity to build doctrines upon metaphors.

FRIENDSHIP is a thing that needs to be cultivated if we would have it come to anything; but enemies like ill weeds will spring up themselves, without our care and toil.

MELANCHOLY is as truly a disease as any other.

THE greatest faults of speech are not those which offend against the rules of eloquence, but of piety and virtue and good manners.

HE that can choose at any time whether he will speak or not (which is certainly in every man's power to do) can choose whether he will swear when he speaks. If he says he does it by custom and habit and when he does not think of it, a very little care and resolution will in a short time cure any man of that custom ; so that it is naturally in every man's power to break off this sin.

WEALTH and riches, that is, an estate above what sufficeth our real occasions and necessities, is in no other sense a ' blessing ' than as it is an opportunity put into our hands, by the providence of God, of doing more good.

HE is not so happy as he may be, who hath not the pleasure of making others so, and of seeing them put into an happy condition by his means, which is the highest pleasure (I had almost said ' pride,' but I may truly say ' glory ') of a good and great mind.[1]

THERE are two things which human nature does more especially desire to be secured against, which are want and contempt ; and riches seem to be a certain remedy against both of these evils.

THE capacity and opportunity of doing greater good is the specious pretence, under which ambition is wont to cover the eager desire of power and greatness.

[1] The thought of Herbert's lines in *The Church Porch* :
' All worldly joys go less
To the one joy of doing kindnesses.'

WE ought to be glad when those that are fit for government and called to it, are willing to take the burden of it upon them : yea, and to be very thankful to them too that they will be at the pains and can have the patience to govern and to live publicly. Therefore it is happy for the world that there are some who are born and bred up to it ; and that custom hath made it easy or at least tolerable to them. Else who that is wise would undertake it, since it is certainly much easier of the two to obey a just and wise government (I had almost said, any government) than to govern justly and wisely ?

NOTHING but necessity, or the hope of doing more good than a man is capable of doing in a private station, can recompense the trouble and uneasiness of a more public and busy life.

MEN are apt to think that they who are in highest places and have the most power, have most liberty to say and do what they please. But it is quite otherwise ; for they have the least liberty, because they are most observed.

POVERTY and contentment do much oftener meet together than a great fortune and a satisfied mind.

No man can judiciously embrace the true religion, unless he be permitted to judge whether that which he embraces be the true religion or not.

BY the happiness of a good education and the merciful providence of God, a great part of many men's virtue consists rather in the good customs they have been bred up to than in the deliberate choice of their own wills.

EVERY little objection appears strong and considerable, which makes against that which men are loth should be true.

IT is usual in Scripture to express the best and most desirable things by *life*.

IF the affections and interests of men were as deeply concerned and as sensibly touched in the truth of mathematical propositions as they are in the principles of morality and religion, we should find that when a proposition stood in their way and lay cross to their interest, though it were never so clearly demonstrated, yet they would raise a dust about it, and make a thousand cavils, and fence even against the evidence of a demonstration.

THE true privilege and advantage of greatness is, to be able to do more good than others.

MANY men's scruples lie almost wholly about obedience to authority and compliance with indifferent customs, but very seldom about the dangers of disobedience and unpeaceableness and rending in pieces the Church of Christ by needless separations and endless divisions.

NOTHING does require greater diligence and attention and care than for a man to become truly and throughly good.

THIS is true love to any one, to do the best for him we can.

As the empty ears of corn are pert and raise up themselves, but those which are big and full droop and hang down their heads, so it is only ignorance that is proud and lifts men up, but true knowledge makes men humble.

THE solicitous vindication of a man's self is, at the best, but an after-game, and for the most part a man had better sit still than to run the hazard of making the matter worse by playing it.

I DO not know whether there be a more delightful sight on this side heaven than to see those who are in eminent place and power, even if they might do whatever they would, yet continually choosing to do what they ought.

It is commonly said that revenge is sweet; but to a calm and considerate mind patience and forgiveness are sweeter and do afford a much more rational and solid and durable revenge.

A MORE glorious victory cannot be gained over another man than this, that when the injury began on his part the kindness should begin on ours.

WHATEVER reason can be assigned why God should provide for the infallible security of our faith is much stronger why an equal provision should be made to secure holiness and obedience of life, because without this, faith cannot infallibly attain its end, which is the salvation of our souls. But this, it is granted, God hath not done; and experience shows it. And therefore it is unreasonable to suppose that he hath done the other.

ALL the revelations of God, as well as the laws of men, go upon this presumption that men are not stark fools, but that they will consider their interest and have some regard to the great concernment of their eternal salvation. And this is as much to secure men from mistake in matters of belief as God hath afforded to keep men from sin in matters of practice. He hath made no effectual and infallible provision that men shall not sin ; and yet it would puzzle any man to give a good reason why God should take more care to secure men against errors in belief than against sin and wickedness in their lives.

RELIGION makes the life of man a wise design, regular and constant to itself, because it unites all our resolutions and actions in one great end. Whereas without religion the life of man is a wild and fluttering and inconsistent thing, without any certain scope and design.

ONE of the first principles of human wisdom in the conduct of our lives, I have ever thought to be this : to have a few intimate friends and to make no enemies, if it be possible, for ourselves.

WE cannot leave the world a better legacy than well-disciplined children.

IF a man do but mix something of religion with all his discourses and be often speaking of God and heavenly things, this passeth for a more than ordinary character of a religious man. And many deceive themselves with it; they have talked of religion so long, till they believe they have it.

Next to the wicked lives of men, nothing is so great a disparagement and weakening to religion as the divisions of Christians.

It seems to be very hard and, if that would do any good, might be just matter of complaint, that we are fallen into so profane and sceptical an age, which takes a pleasure and a pride in unravelling almost all the received principles both of religion and reason, so that we are put many times to prove those things which can hardly be made plainer than they are of themselves.

There are two things in which men, in other things wise enough, do usually miscarry : in putting off the making of their wills and their repentance, till it be too late.

No man makes any remarkable change in his life, so as to cross his inclinations and custom, without an express resolution.

Resolution is no strange and extraordinary thing; it is one of the most common acts that belong to us as we are men. But we do not ordinarily apply it to the best purposes. It is not so ordinary for men to resolve to be good as to resolve to be rich and great, not so common for men to resolve against sin as to resolve against poverty and suffering. It is not so usual for men to resolve to keep a good conscience as to keep a good place.

WE have many powerful enemies, but we are much more in danger of treachery from within than of assault from without. All the power of our enemies could not destroy us if we were but true to ourselves.[1]

POWER and necessity go together. When men are hard pressed, they find a power which they thought they had not ; and when it comes to the push, men can do that which they see plainly they either must do or be ruined for ever.

ZEAL is an edge-tool, which children in understanding should not meddle withal ; and yet it most frequently possesseth the weakest minds.

THE best way in the world for a man to seem to

---

[1] Perhaps an unconscious reminiscence of the last lines in Shakespeare's *King John* :

'Nought shall make us rue,
If England to itself do rest but true.'

be any thing, is really to be what he would seem to be.[1]

EVERY man will not take upon him to be a physician or a lawyer, to prescribe medicines in dangerous cases and to give counsel to men in knotty and difficult points about their estates ; but every man thinks himself fit enough to be rich, and sufficiently qualified to manage a great estate, if he can but get it—when perhaps there are few things in the world which men are more insufficient for than to wield and govern a great fortune, nor wherein there is a greater danger of miscarriage. It is not everybody's talent to be wealthy and wise, rich and innocent.

IT is unhappy for men that they believe so well, when they live so ill.

SURELY it is quite a wrong way for any man to go about, by the mere strength and subtlety of his reason and wit, tho' never so great, to interpret an ancient book without understanding and considering the historical occasion of it, which is the only thing that can give true light to it.

GOD doth, as it were, by afflictions throw men

---

[1] From the great sermon on Sincerity (see above, p. 176).

upon their backs, to make them look up to heaven.

MAN is an ambitious creature and vain above all things, so vain as not only to be covetous of praise but even patient of flattery. And the best of men lie too open, on this blind side of human nature. And therefore God, who knows our frame and how apt dust and ashes are to be proud, hath in his wise and merciful providence so disposed things that good men are seldom exposed to the full force of so strong a temptation. And for this reason he lets loose envious and malicious tongues, to detract from good men, for a check to the vanity of human nature and to keep their virtue safe under the protection of humility.

WHEN a man hath done all the good turns he can and endeavoured to oblige every man, and not only to live inoffensively but exemplarily, he is fairly dealt with and comes off upon good terms, if he can but escape the ill words of men for doing well and obtain a pardon for those things which truly deserve praise.

EVERY man hath greater assurance that God is good and just than he can have of any subtle speculations about predestination and the decrees of God.

MEN may speak like angels and yet do like devils.

BECAUSE we are familiar to ourselves, we cannot be strange and wonderful to ourselves; but the great miracle of the world is the mind of man, and the contrivance of it an eminent instance of God's wisdom.

WE cannot glorify and honour God more than by entertaining great thoughts of his mercy.

I WILL not pronounce anything concerning the impossibility of a death-bed repentance, but I am sure that it is very difficult and, I believe, very rare.

IGNORANCE hath had the good fortune to meet with great patrons in the world, and to be extolled as if it were the mother of devotion. Of superstition I grant it is, and of this we see plentiful proof, among those who are so careful to preserve and cherish it; but that true piety and devotion should spring from it is as unlikely as that darkness should produce light.

THE true ground of most men's prejudice against the Christian doctrine is because they have no mind to obey it.

To what purpose should the providence of God take so much care to preserve our religion to us, when we make no better use of it for the direction and government of our lives, when it serves most of us only to talk of it, and too many amongst us to talk against it ?

METHINKS there is no sadder sign of the decay of Christianity, and of the little power and influence that the gospel hath upon us, than that there is so little regard had by Christians to these moral duties, which, because ' moral ' (however men may slight that word), are therefore of eternal and indispensable obligation, having their foundation in the nature of God.

SURELY that church is not to be heard, which will not hear reason.[1]

THIS may probably be one reason why many men who are observed to be sufficiently dull in other matters, yet can talk profanely and speak against religion with some kind of salt and smartness, because religion is the thing that frets them,

---

[1] His friend Whichcote once asked : ' Do I dishonour my faith or do any wrong to it, to tell the world that my mind and understanding are satisfied in it ? I have no reason against it ; yea, the highest and purest reason is for it. What doth God speak to, but my reason ? And should not that which is spoken to, hear ? '

and as in other things so in this, *vexatio dat intellectum,* the inward trouble and vexation of their minds gives them some kind of wit and sharpness in rallying upon religion. Their consciences are galled by it, and this makes them winch and fling as if they had some mettle.

Sin is a base and ill-natured thing, and renders a man not so apt to be affected with the injuries he hath offered to God as with the mischief which is likely to fall upon himself.

Tempting others to sin is in scripture called murder. *Whosoever committeth sin is of the devil,* but whosoever tempts others to sin is a sort of devil himself.

When we say, God hath revealed anything, we must be ready to prove it, or else we say nothing. If we turn off reason here, we level the best religion in the world with the wildest and most absurd enthusiasms.

We have all the reason in the world to believe that the goodness and justice of God is such as to make nothing necessary to be believed by any man which, by the help of due instruction, may not be made sufficiently plain to a common understanding.

THE goodness of God in sparing us is in some respect greater than his goodness in creating us; because he had no provocation not to make us, but we provoke him daily to destroy us.

MEN have hardened their faces in this degenerate age, and these gentle restraints of modesty which governed and kept men in order heretofore signify nothing nowadays; blushing is out of fashion, and shame is ceased from among the children of men.

THERE is nothing many times wanting to take away prejudice and to extinguish hatred and ill-will, but an opportunity for men to see and understand one another; by which they will quickly perceive that they are not such monsters as they have been represented one to another at a distance.

IT were unfit that so excellent and glorious a reward as the gospel promises should stoop down like fruit upon a full-grown bough, to be plucked by every idle and wanton hand.

MEN expect that religion should cost them no pains, that happiness should drop into their laps without any design and endeavour on their part, and that, after they have done what they please while they live, God should snatch them up to heaven when they die. But tho' *the commandments of God be not grievous*, yet it is fit to let men know that they are not thus easy.

I CANNOT believe that force is a fit argument to produce faith ; no man shall ever persuade me, no not the bishop of Meaux [1] with all his eloquence, that prisons and tortures, dragoons and the galleys, are proper means to convince the understanding, and either Christian or human methods of converting men to the true religion.

I THINK there is no reason to doubt but that the blessed spirits above, who continually *behold the face of their Father*, are still writing after this copy which is here propounded to us, and endeavouring to be *perfect as their Father which is in heaven is perfect*, still aspiring after a nearer and more perfect resemblance of God, whose goodness and mercy is far beyond and before that of any creature, that they may be for ever approaching nearer to it and yet never overtake it.

THE queen of Sheba thought Solomon's servants happy in having the opportunity, by standing con-

---

[1] Bossuet's approval and enforcement of the 'pious edict' which harried the Huguenots was resented far beyond his own country.

tinually before him, to hear his wisdom ; but in
the other world it shall be a happiness to Solomon
himself and to the wisest and greatest persons
that ever were in this world, to stand before this
great King to admire his wisdom and to behold
his glory.

WHEN we come to heaven we shall be ready to
say of it, as the queen of Sheba did of Solomon's
wisdom and prosperity, that *half of it hath not been
told us*, that the felicities and glories of that state do
far exceed all the fame which we had heard of them
in this world.   For who can say how great a good
God is, and how happy he who is the fountain of
happiness can make those souls that love him and
those whom he loves ?

WHO can tell what employment God may have
for us in the next life ? [1]

---

[1] This thought became common in last century. In his Journal for
10th December 1825, Scott wrote : ' They have a poor idea of the Deity,
and the rewards which are destined for the just made perfect, who can only
adopt the literal sense of an eternal concert—a never-ending Birthday Ode.
I rather suppose there should be understood some commission from the
Highest, some duty to discharge with the applause of a satisfied conscience.'
' My idea of heaven is the perpetual ministry of one soul to another '
(Tennyson).   And Matthew Arnold's lines to his father, beginning :

> ' O strong soul, by what shore
> Tarriest thou now ? '

are too familiar to need quotation.

IF he hath promised to make us happy, tho' he hath not particularly declared to us wherein this happiness shall consist, yet we may trust him that made us, to find out ways to make us happy, and may believe that he who made us, without our knowledge or desire, is able to make us happy beyond them both.[1]

[1] Addison, in the *Spectator* (n. 600), refers to this argument admiringly.